SACRED SILENCE

AN AWAKENING EXPERIENCE

*A journey out of the mind and into the void of silence,
the gateway to unconditional love, universal
wisdom, and infinite abundance!*

NATALIE PRECI

BALBOA.PRESS

A DIVISION OF HAY HOUSE

Balboa Press books may be ordered through booksellers or by contacting:

Balboa Press
A Division of Hay House
1663 Liberty Drive
Bloomington, IN 47403
www.balboapress.com.au
AU TFN: 1 800 844 925 (Toll Free inside Australia)
AU Local: (02) 8310 7086 (+61 2 8310 7086 from outside Australia)

Print information available on the last page.

ISBN: 978-1-9822-9032-0 (sc)
ISBN: 978-1-9822-9033-7 (e)

Balboa Press rev. date: 07/15/2022

To Jonathan Barry (Fritzler)—without your love, patience, and belief in me, this book might never have happened. Following my awakening experience, I reached out to you, and you gently guided me to an open door and inspired me to walk through. Your presence alone has taught me so much, as has your generosity of spirit and huge open heart. I will forever be honoured to have crossed your path and have a front row seat to your God-given gifts and genius mind. Thank you, Brother, for always believing in me and giving me the tools to believe in myself.

CONTENTS

Acknowledgements xiii

Introduction xv

Chapter 1   Who Am I?... 1

   1.1   Search for Self 1

   1.2   Saviour Within.. 4

   1.3   My Awakening 5

Chapter 2   I Am Who I Say I Am............................. 9

   2.1   And I Say 9

   2.2   The Power of *I Am* 9

   2.3   *I Am*—The Name Ascribed to God........................11

   2.4   Vibrational Frequency of Words and Thought............13

   2.5   Love Is at The Core 14

   2.6   Transformation...15

Chapter 3   Rewind—1982 16

   3.1   When I Was Seven Years Old 16

   3.2   Sticks and Stones May Break My Bones...................18

   3.3   Compartmentalising Trauma............................19

   3.4   The Baby Elephant 20

   3.5   I Found Jesus!...23

Chapter 4   Beyond the Constraints of Religion **25**

  4.1   A New Way of Thinking 25

  4.2   My Christian Interpretation of God 27

  4.3   Fear Tactics 27

  4.4   The Devil, the Scapegoat 29

  4.5   Justifiable Punishment for Sin 30

  4.6   Am I God's Faulty Merchandise? 30

  4.7   Back and Forth from Conviction to Anarchist 31

  4.8   The Trouble with the Word *God* 33

  4.9   Good Versus Evil 35

  4.10   Who Is God? 35

  4.11   The Oneness of God 37

  4.12   What Is Eternity? 39

  4.13   Facing Our Own Demons 40

  4.14   Religion Is Not God—God Is Not Religion 40

Chapter 5   Living in the Matrix **42**

  5.1   Is Anything Real? 42

Chapter 6   The Rabbit Hole of World Conspiracies **45**

  6.1   Who Controls the World? 45

  6.2   Global Depopulation—A Moral Dilemma 48

  6.3   The Darkness of Evil Intent 49

  6.4   It's All Virtual Reality 50

Chapter 7   Coming Off Autopilot **51**

  7.1   Living in the Fog of Denial 51

  7.2   Where Was My Moral Dessert? 52

  7.3   The Plight of a Hopeless Romantic and Dreamer 54

  7.4   Where Is Everyone? 55

  7.5   If You Will Change, My Life Will Be Perfect! 57

  7.6   Liberate Yourself 59

7.7   Pulling the Plug on Social Media.................................59
7.8   Time to Get Real 61

Chapter 8   The Ego versus the True Self 63

8.1   Who Are You?...63
8.2   The Ego 64
8.3   Manifestations of the Ego 67
8.4   The True Self 74

Chapter 9   Becoming the Best Version of Yourself................ 76

9.1   Are You the Best You Can Be? 76
9.2   Dropping All Masks and Facades 77
9.3   The World's Youth, Obsessed with Self-Image...........78
9.4   Love Your Body—All of It!...79
9.5   Let the Real You Shine 79
9.6   Your Authentic Self...80
9.7   Fight or Flight Mode..81
9.8   The Scars We Bear Reveal Our Strength.....................82
9.9   Resistance to Change 85

Chapter 10 Addiction 87

10.1   My Personal Journey into Addiction 87
10.2   Why I Chose Drugs..87
10.3   Will Power Is for the Undisciplined............................90
10.4   Deceptive Self-Justification and Convenient Labels ...91
10.5   Forgive Yourself First, Then Face the Truth................92
10.6   A Lifeline in Disguise 92
10.7   Do You Know Someone Suffering from Addiction?...94
10.8   Your Addiction Doesn't Define You 94
10.9   The Forgotten Addict 95
10.10 The High-Functioning Addict......................................96
10.11 Social Responsibility 97

Chapter 11 The Confines of Society **98**

11.1   Where Has Our Freedom Gone? 98
11.2   Traditional Schooling and Education..........................99
11.3   Our Choice or a Product of Our Birthplace? 101

Chapter 12 What Is Reality? **103**

12.1   Reality Is an Illusion..103
12.2   Flat Earth Theory 104
12.3   The Scientific Theory of Quantum Physics 107
12.4   Reticular Activating System 109

Chapter 13 Social Isolation **111**

13.1   Global Epidemic 111
13.2   Open Up the Lines of Communication 112
13.3   Technology—Friend or Foe?.....................................113
13.4   Emotional Isolation..114
13.5   The Upside of Isolation..115

Chapter 14 Overcoming the Misconception of Failure **117**

14.1   Failure Is Not a Four-Letter Word............................117
14.2   Pity Party for One 118
14.3   Failure Identifies Our Weakness 119
14.4   Personal Growth and Development 119

Chapter 15 Chasing the Wind **120**

15.1   Materialism 120
15.2   Madness and Folly..122
15.3   Too Busy to Live 123

Chapter 16 Defying the Odds **124**

16.1   The Odds Are Never Too Great 124
16.2   Two Brothers—One Alcoholic Father 125
16.3   You Have A Choice...125

Chapter 17 How to Repel Negativity and Toxic People 126

   17.1   Energy-Sucking Vampires.....................................126
   17.2   Defining Your Boundaries.....................................127
   17.3   Remaining Steadfast in Your Resolve.....................128
   17.4   If You Are the Smartest One in the Room.................128

Chapter 18 Discovering True Happiness.....................130

   18.1   Letting Go of Unhappiness....................................130
   18.2   Fear of Being Happy 131

Chapter 19 The Creative Forces of Necessity 133

   19.1   When We Hit Rock Bottom....................................133
   19.2   Are You Going to Walk Or Run?..............................134
   19.3   The Hidden Treasures Within 135
   19.4   Don't Wait Until It's Too Late 136
   19.5   Who Will You Let Steal Your Dreams? 137

Chapter 20 Rewriting a Painful Past 138

   20.1   Factory Reset..138
   20.2   Memories 139
   20.3   Change Your Emotional Response to Your Past........139

Chapter 21 How to Create a New Paradigm 141

   21.1   A New Chapter in Your Life...................................141

Chapter 22 Laws of the Universe 144

   22.1   Law of Attraction..144

Chapter 23 Power of Thought 147

   23.1   Our Thoughts Are What We Become 147
   23.2   A Powerful Message—Rubin "Hurricane" Carter 147
   23.3   Our Thoughts Can Set Us Free 149

Chapter 24 Thought-Inspired Action....................................**150**

24.1   The Thought Cycle.......................................150

24.2   Changing Your Thoughts............................152

24.3   Changing Your Actions...............................153

24.4   Changing Your Emotions...........................154

Chapter 25 Affirmations and Meditation....................**155**

25.1   Positive Affirmations..................................155

25.2   The Lies We Tell Ourselves 158

25.3   Morning Affirmations.................................159

25.4   The Art of Meditation 160

Chapter 26 New Life Begins....................................**162**

26.1   Relinquishing My Ego Self........................162

ACKNOWLEDGEMENTS

Orlando and Eliavah, my children

To my best friends and greatest loves—my children, Orlando and Eliavah. You have been brave beyond your years, the bright lights on my darkest days. Even in the innocence of youth, your innate capacity for unconditional love, empathy, and compassion have proven to be your greatest gifts. You have both been my wise council, somehow finding the right words to comfort me in time of distress, never allowing me to give up on myself.

Orlando and Eliavah, you are beautiful souls, and I'm forever grateful to experience this journey of life with you. Living in the moment—in happiness, joy, and peace—I will savour every smile and wipe every tear as it falls, loving you unconditionally and guiding you into your soul purpose. My love for you has no bounds and is eternal. You are my champions, as I will forever be yours.

Rachelle Hamilton-Cohen, my mother

You are the most beautiful woman in the world. Thank you for giving me life and nurturing my true self. You never asked me to change and accepted all versions of me without question or judgement. Your love and unwavering support will never be forgotten in this physical plane or the spiritual.

As your mind continues to ascend as your memories of this world fade, your laughter, joy, and soft heart will be forever remembered by all those who have been blessed to have known you. I love you, Mum, without measure, and I can't wait to meet you again in the spirit. Your presence will always remain in the hearts of the countless people whose lives you have touched with your effortless grace, kindness, compassion, and witty sense of humour.

The footprint you have left on this world will be remembered, and your legacy will live on in your children, your grandchildren, and their grandchildren. I will make sure of it. This world was never meant for one as beautiful as you!

Preng (Joshua) Preci

Thank you for your input, inspiration, and support in completing this book. You have been instrumental in forcing me to look within myself for the love and acceptance I sought and found. As we continue our journeys and raise our beautiful children my hope is that we find peace within the eternal now and acceptance of what is.

Angeline Prince and Leanna Tucker, my big sisters

I love you both so deeply and respect and honour our differences. As we all grow and evolve individually and come to accept each other for who we are, our unbreakable bond is strengthened. You have both been there for me at different times in my life, to support me, encourage me and provide me with loving guidance for which I am eternally grateful. I hope this book makes you proud.

My Soul Tribe

To those I have met and those I have yet to meet. You all have an intrinsic place in my heart. You have been my friends when I've felt alone, my lifeline in distress, my wise counsel, a compassionate ear without judgement, an inspiration, a family, and a support system that gives me so much love and joy. My gratitude is overflowing. This book is for you. Love and light to you all. Namaste.

INTRODUCTION

This work is dedicated to those who find themselves at a crossroads in life, wanting more but without the tools with which to achieve it. It is for those who have tried everything they know how to change their lives and still find themselves trapped in a cycle of repetitive negative experiences, emotions, or circumstance.

We all face adversities and challenges throughout our lives that can cripple us if we don't identify the lessons they present. Life is not just series of highs and lows but the totality of the journey through which we evolve from resistance to life into complete surrender to what is.

When we exit the mind and enter consciousness, we find inner wisdom and understanding of who we really are—our true self and our connection to all things in the universe. *True self* is a non-concentrated conscious energy field vibrating at various distinctive frequencies of the universe, flowing with infinite potential and possibilities, and existing beyond all space, time, names, and conceptual form.

This is the story of how I found myself no longer wanting to live. I had resigned myself to the fact that I might never know true happiness. Even if it did exist, I was just too tired to continue my search; my strength was all but consumed. I believed my heart would forever be weighed down with sadness and my soul overcome by hopelessness. I just wanted to stop thinking, stop the external noise, and quiet the voices inside my head that prevented me from ever experiencing peace.

But then, in a moment, in the blinking of the eye, something extraordinary happened. My brain involuntarily surrendered. My thoughts became null. My emotions shut down. My feelings were now unidentifiable. My mind was finally succumbing to the overload of information. Everything became quiet, and there was nothing but silence—a stillness that permeated to the depths of my soul.

Yet in this stillness, I felt peace. This peace bought forth joy. The joy manifested into surreal happiness. The happiness revealed my true self. I was grateful to be alive. This wasn't going to be my end but my beginning.

The ever-increasing number of souls that endure the incomprehensible devastation and hopelessness of a life lacking any true wisdom of their worth and importance to the world saddens me to the core. The World Health Organisation estimates that each year, approximately 1 million people die from suicide, which represents a global mortality rate of 16 people per 100,000 or one death every 40 seconds. It is predicted that by 2022, the rate of death will increase to one every 20 seconds.

Before we go on this journey together, I ask that you free your mind of any preconceived ideas and beliefs, allowing yourself to be open to a new way of understanding. It is not my goal to teach you anything that you don't already know. It is not my wisdom to impart but the wisdom of the universe, which is accessible to all. My hope is to help you tap into its awesome power by recognising the blockages in your own life that may be preventing you from harnessing it as I share my own experiences along the way. I pray that by the end of this book, you will come to the fullness of understanding that you are in this very moment already divine perfection and infinite, untapped potential.

This book is not the result of some casual musings but the crucial insights I have passionately sought my entire life. Learn how to reprogram your subconscious paradigm to free yourself from negative beliefs that hold you back from living a life of limitless possibility. Our mindset determines our experiences, and we are in control and the master of all. By understanding the laws of quantum mechanics and their creative power, we can bring into existence the very reality we desire. The moment we take positive action evolving from a positive thought, we have affected our future reality.

This is not a road of tough terrain but an easy path to great victory. You must be willing to take back command of your thoughts and to take up the reins of your own destiny. Your mind can be your most powerful asset or your greatest foe, guiding your dreams or burying you in self-doubt. The choice is *always* yours.

A great man, James Allen, famous for his book *What a Man Thinketh*, first published in 1903, eloquently expresses insight into the most fundamental nature of man. The title is influenced by a verse in the Bible from the Book of Proverbs (23:7, KJV): "For as he thinketh in his heart, so is he." His words flow like honey from the pages as he effortlessly describes the condition of the human spirit. One passage from his book echoes the verity of such notions of the power of thought to create reality:

> The aphorism, "As a man thinketh in his heart so is he," not only embraces the whole of a man's being but is so comprehensive as to reach out to every condition and circumstance of his life. A man is literally what he thinks, his character being the complete sum of all his thoughts.

I am truly honoured and grateful for this opportunity to share my story and reach out to you in the fullness of love and hope.

CHAPTER 1

WHO AM I?

Knowing yourself is the beginning of all wisdom.—Aristotle

1.1 Search for Self

Who am I? That is a question I have laboured to find a satisfactory answer to my entire life. It was an agonising pursuit of irrefutable evidence to support my vague and naive ideals about my true nature and the space I occupy in the world. I looked to everyone and in everything for the answers I so desperately sought, in a dire need to be free from the perplexity and conflict of my mind.

At forty-two years of age, just after New Year's Eve of 2018, I was despondent and unmoved by the frivolous and mindless celebrations of the common man. I was not one for idle gatherings of people who didn't possess my intrinsic need to conceptualise the meaning of life and self in their most raw state.

A long road of unrealised dreams, unfulfilled expectations, deep sorrow, rejection, affliction, misfortune, and trauma had left me with a grave disdain and contempt for the world around me and the sheeplike beings contained within. I had grown so weary living a life on the extreme borderline of existence, a life so meaningless it was difficult to distinguish it from death itself. It caused me to consider that death may be better than the bitter sting of life.

I felt I had gotten to the end of the road, with no place left to turn to escape from the prison of my thoughts. I had exhausted all my options for assistance. I had given it everything I had, time and time again, to reverse the effects of my malaise. My strength was now depleted, my hope all but lost.

I'd thrown myself back and forth on the mercy of God too many times to count, escaping into my addiction, praying every prayer, worshipping on my knees till the early morning, delving to the depths of rabbit hole conspiracies, studying the signs in the heavens, considering ancient religions, begging family and friends to acknowledge my pain, and seeking counsel from all I knew. But my cries went unanswered, and my silent tears fell without testimony to their cause.

My anguish went unacknowledged, and the loathsome reality of my condition neglected to incite any compassion. I had replayed my life over and over. It was like a horror movie as I recounted the misery and pain I suffered at my own hands and that which was inflicted on me by others without reason or remorse.

I thought back to almost every encounter I'd had throughout my life and could see they lacked depth and remained, not by choice, superficial in nature. These haunting memories of my life remained trapped in my mind like a torture chamber of unquantifiable truths, entwined with the silent, unceasing conversations of past encounters that tormented me with their hostile verbiage.

The incessant chattering taking place in my head was a desperate attempt to dispel the conflict of my mind. It was deafening. I began to question my sanity. Was I the victim of a multiple personality disorder? I often felt as if there were several personalities arguing, bickering, and competing for dominance within my mind's hierarchy. Monologues played out with contradicting versions of myself, all curated by me, serving my different needs.

If you could have experienced just one minute in my thoughts, you would easily conceive the woe and discontent of my spirit and start looking for the exit from the hell in which you had found yourself.

> What a liberation to realize that the "voice in my head" is not who I am. Who am I then? The one who sees that.
>
> **Eckhart Tolle, *The Power of Now***

I had become fake, not knowing how to exist being anything else. I was proficient in the art of disguise, plastering a smile on my face every moment, feigning inner happiness. I was becoming just a conjecture of others' expectations.

The sheer agony of contemplating another forty years of life like this was unbearable. The weight of my predicament felt like heavy chains encircling my heart. It seemed nothing could release me from the pain as they constricted their grip daily, getting tighter and tighter, until every breath I took became laboured. My heart was slowly dying, broken, and beaten.

The dull constant ache was insufferable. At times, I prayed for the day the pressure would prove too great and my heart would simply cease beating, letting me slowly fade into unconscious oblivion, the first stop before death, my exit from this world being the ultimate freedom from my excruciating existence. I was no longer concerned for my religious beliefs or the fear they had instilled in me of heaven and hell. I thought I'd take my chances with the devil. It couldn't be worse than my reality.

I'd spent my whole life in search of truth, only to be left drowning in a sea of lies and deceit. My search for truth had left me so confused, my spiritual compass was spinning out of control. I could not find my way back to true north. I was like a leaf blowing in the wind, swirling around, up and down, without purpose or direction. Even the mere thought of once again trying to critically evaluate another theory on the meaning of life sent me spiralling into hopelessness and despair.

Was my persistent search for higher knowledge of higher self in vain, or had I just overcomplicated the purpose of my life? Maybe it's as simple as "After birth, death is inevitable, so just have fun in between." I have known many atheists in my life, and it seemed their lack of any spiritual faith allowed them to live with a carefree abandon, never having to question right or wrong. They lived in the moment, not having to worry about tomorrow.

There were periods in my life when I set aside my faith. I craved a reprieve from the ever-present uncertainty of my deservedness of eternal life, every moment striving to be deemed worthy by imposing upon myself unrealistic restrictions and rules that I continuously struggled to uphold. My inability to maintain any significant change in my life expressed itself as failure, causing feelings of self-hatred. I could not achieve any degree of peace while mentally trying to derive an answer to a question I could no longer articulate.

Where would I find the key to my freedom, which now lay buried amongst a multitude of conflicting beliefs, doctrines, and ideals that had been programmed or learnt throughout my life, when I was no longer able to separate fact from fiction? The end of the road was before me; I sensed it. I knew it was close. Any moment could be my last before I dropped dead from the anguish of my despair.

On the second of January, 2018, two days into an existential crisis, I couldn't sleep; I couldn't eat. My heaving sobs refused to be contained. All I could do was cry out and pray for a way free from the burden of such mental and emotional duress.

What could release me from my mental captivity and physical actuality? My once endless stamina had been consumed, exhausted, extinguished. I had lost the will to keep fighting.

1.2   Saviour Within

Could it possibly be that I had failed to acknowledge the truth that was within me and with me my whole life? That I am the creator of my reality? That I am the author of my own life? That the myriad of my life experiences, thoughts, and emotions were the aggregate total of everything I had become and what I used to define myself?

Was this understanding the key to awakening in me the truth that had been so long hidden? If so, I would not be disheartened to realise that my life was an actuality of my own making. On the contrary, I would be overwhelmed with a sense of gratitude, owing to the realisation that I was the sole custodian of my thoughts, which had the power to keep me locked in or the power to set me free. My life didn't have to continue in a perpetual state of confusion and self-doubt but could be reshaped and moulded by the power of my mind. It was an understanding that all that I thought I was, was not me at all.

1.3   My Awakening

The path of awakening is not about becoming who you are. Rather it is about unbecoming who you are not.

Albert Schweitzer

My awakening happened in an instant. Every thought that had become an object of confusion was simply gone. The ceaseless multitude of conflicting thoughts literally dissipated, erased from my mind. I didn't have a thought at all.

I found myself in a catatonic, trance-like state. The mass of thoughts that had hijacked my mind were gone, leaving a void in their wake. It was as if something deep inside me had ordered a forced shutdown of my conscious mind in an act of self-preservation and survival.

This was the mental breakdown I had feared for years, and yet within this void, I felt complete control. How could this be? If my mind had ceased to operate and was no longer the controlling force of my emotional and mental state, then what was the source of my sense of well-being and strength in that moment?

Once my mind had been involuntarily shut down, an alternate source of power was initiated, flowing with an electrifying current of high-voltage energy. Where had this come from, and why had it been so obscured from my understanding prior to this moment?

The energy carried with it wisdom: knowledge pertaining to the universe and my identity. This was the key to my freedom, unlocking the door to my mind's eye, answering all questions ever asked in silence. It was the absolute awareness of self and completeness of love.

Now, before me, I could see my divine purpose—not a life purpose, not a passion, not a dream, but a state of being. It's difficult to explain, but it was as if my individual self, being disconnected and removed from my true nature and the world, was absorbed into the oneness of the universe, and I felt connected again.

There were no more unanswered questions; it was as if someone did a high-speed download of all universal knowledge and wisdom that left nothing up to chance or open for debate. There were no holes in the theory, nothing that could be misinterpreted. It was so simple, so basic, that when I awakened to it, I couldn't understand how I hadn't experienced it before. This wisdom and understanding was delivered in silence. It did not cloud my thinking or overwhelm me with words. It was gentle and subtle, yet complete.

Several weeks following this enlightenment, I came to understand I had always been connected to my higher self and source consciousness. However, I failed to identify its origin or pay heed to the signs it often yielded. I had searched my mind, enquired of my soul, and looked to the physical environment being the home of my egoic self, never able to break through the veil separating me from this higher dimension of consciousness.

Now, holding full power of attorney over my mind, I instinctively knew I first had to bring to an abrupt halt any further descent into depression by arresting all negative thoughts, beliefs, and emotions. You see, we are not so much physical but thought, not so much flesh but feeling. What makes you who you are is the point of conscious awareness from which you experience life—how your focus, emotions, and beliefs influence and control these experiences and the way your mind processes the information. Every thought you have ever purposefully entertained or let seep into your subconscious has shaped and moulded you through your life, whether you have been consciously aware of it or not.

Once able to procure the power of my higher self by drawing on this yet unknown energy source, I could intentionally slow down the rapid firing of unsolicited thoughts and re-establish cognitive command over my mind. I experienced a sense of peace that I had only believed to be a tale of ancient mythology and idle fantasy: a peace that gave refuge to my soul.

A state of being calm, peaceful and untroubled.

Serenity

Serenity is a state which, if having hue, could not be limited to one shade but be a kaleidoscope of iridescent colour. The indistinct, overlapping voices in my mind had finally quieted, and I sank into a silence comparable to euphoric bliss.

The silence permitted my ears to hear sounds that had for so long been blocked from my recognition. For the first time, I could hear the drumming of my heart as it beat within my chest. I could hear the wind as it subtly whisked about my face. I could make out the distant melodies of the birds singing far above, sounds that had been inaudible prior to that moment. This all may seem a little corny, but it is the only way I can describe the experience and do it justice.

The grass appeared greener and highly contrasted against the vivid blue of the sky. There was beauty all around me; I could see it, smell it, touch it, and feel it, and not just in nature but in inanimate objects. I was now viewing all matter with a renewed appreciation for the miracle it is. Despite my spiritual walk-through of Christianity for many years, I had yet to experience a rebirth into the heavenly nature of the world around me with such enlightened presence.

The quandary of "Who am I?" was not so much a question anymore that could be answered with defined limitations but an awareness. My once blurred vision of self was now in clear focus. My eyes were opened to the power I contained within, that was me, though also greater than me. There was no going back. My consciousness had awakened to the truth of my existence and spoken to me, saying, *I am …*

CHAPTER 2

I AM WHO I SAY I AM

2.1   And I Say …

I am love! I am God! I am gratefulness! I am peace! I am strength! I am forgiveness! I am abundant! I am united yet divided!

I am divided yet constitute the formation of the single highest source of all universal consciousness. I am singular, but I am plural, existing independently and cooperatively, simultaneously.

Before condemning me for blasphemy, understand I do not claim to be or intend to imply that I am the omniscience, omnipotence, or omnipresent source of all creation, just to say that I am, as you are, a sub-creation formed out of its very conscious thought.

2.2   The Power of *I Am*

These two little words, *I am*, leverage the complete creative influence over the blueprint of our very reality. They are the most consequential words that have ever and will ever exist in the collective consciousness of humankind and God. The power of *I am* is the sole determiner that establishes the path of our destiny; the mere act of thinking them influences our fate. The subsequent word, spoken or thought, creates, contributes to, or compounds that which you already believe.

I think therefore I am.

Rene Descartes

Discerning the potency of these words, having mindful respect for their creative power, restrains their negative implications so one does not to fall victim to them. The utterance of negative words that follow *I am* serve only to defame and vilify the ethos of oneself and is an ungracious act that would be undeserving of a stranger. Yet when statements like *I am not worthy, I am a sinner, I am unlucky, I am in lack, I am depressed, I am old,* or *I am weak* come from the mouth or thoughts of those in whom they are directed, then this is what they become.

The words that follow *I am* form an effigy from the substance contained within the soul of a man, that is the man. Because the seed that is sown within the heart of a man is nurtured to maturity by his own thoughts, it awaits its opportunity to be expressed in character and action, whether to his benefit or detriment.

The desires of the heart are first planted in the consciousness of mankind by thought. Our thoughts are made visible in the physical manifestation of our character and life circumstance. We need to take inventory of what follows the *I am* from the second we open our eyes, entering consciousness each morning. The first words we allow to be circulated in our thoughts should be ones of gratitude.

Just imagine how your day might flow if you start by giving thanks for all the blessings you do have and affirm them with conviction: *I am blessed, I am talented, I am strong, I am healthy, I am rich, I am beautiful, I am young, I am happy, I am joyful,* or whatever affirmations you feel will start your day off on an unshakable footing. But it is not just to recite such affirmations but to embody the emotions and feelings that go along with them.

To think is one thing, but to experience is another. Our subconscious mind has no ability to distinguish actual events from our imagination. When we imagine a scenario being played out, our mind conceives it as reality.

The ultimate truth of who you are is not I am this or I am that, but I Am.

Eckhart Tolle, *The Power of Now*

So command into life today what it is that you want to experience through clear visualisation and faith that you already have it. Don't wait until tomorrow, as tomorrow is nothing more than our mind's ability to project expectations beyond the present moment. The only time that exists is now, this minute, this hour, this day. Tomorrow is not promised. Seize this moment to declare the *I am*s you wish to become and the emotions you wish to experience.

2.3   *I Am*—The Name Ascribed to God

I Am is the name God ascribed to himself throughout the scriptures of the Bible. Probably the best-known usage of *I Am* occurs in Exodus 3, beginning in verse 13:

> [13]And Moses said unto God, Behold, when I come unto the children of Israel, and shall say unto them, The God of your fathers hath sent me unto you; and they shall say to me, What is his name? what shall I say unto them?[14]And God said unto Moses, I AM THAT I AM: and he said, Thus shalt thou say unto the children of Israel, I AM hath sent me unto you.15And God said moreover unto Moses, Thus shalt thou say unto the children of Israel, The LORD God of your fathers, the God of Abraham, the God of

Isaac, and the God of Jacob, hath sent me unto you:
this is my name for ever, and this is my memorial unto
all generations.—Exodus 3:13-15, KJV

You see, God professed within scripture the simplicity and absoluteness of his Being. But why these two words? What makes these two words so complete in their most basic nature that they can encompass the completeness of God's divinity and character? Because what followed them was the terms in which he defined himself!

The term *I Am* appears in the Bible 719 times: 508 times in the Old Testament and 211 times in the New Testament. Understanding the relevance and importance placed on these two words within scripture, how then do they serve us in our comprehension of self and the intended objective of their purpose in our lives?

The interpretation of scripture that is upheld in modern religion of the true nature and entity of God has been sorely miscommunicated. Whether due to the multiple translations of scripture from the ancient Greek and Arabic texts or through the countless interpretations by theologians throughout the ages, we have failed to represent the authentic embodiment of the great *I am* and our connection to him.

There are hundreds of occurrences in the biblical scriptures where God uses the words *I am* to express himself and declare the nature of his purpose. Is man's purpose consistent with that of God? If we are an expression of God and made in his image, then it is logical to assume we reflect that which God is. A representation of a pure heart, pure thoughts, and pure action which bears witness to the God within.

But this is not humanity's default nature. It has become self-important, identifying with religion, and associating it as a spiritual anchor. However, the anchor to our true spirituality comes from the depths of our true self. We are all connected to this anchor rope but struggle to follow it to the greatest depths.

Every inch we make towards our centre, we come up against the darkness of our inner self, demons from the past wanting us to remain in torment, our ego wanting to keep us in bondage to our programmed beliefs, our minds overwhelming us with thoughts. No wonder we never make it to the deepest depths of our true spirituality. To do so we must fear nothing, ignore the demons, push aside our egoistic beliefs, and quiet our minds. Only then will we learn what cannot be taught.

It is a journey into the present moment. No past, no future, no physical self, just you. This is your moment of awakening to who you really are, feeling a oneness and acceptance for all things.

2.4   Vibrational Frequency of Words and Thought

Our audible words and thoughts have a vibrational energy attached to them that seeks out compatible frequencies in the cosmos of electromagnetic fields that operate continuously, seen or unseen. Like attracts like. This is not a term that should be casually dismissed without first contemplating its scientific validity within the framework of the laws that govern all matter and consciousness.

Our thoughts have an energy signature that syncs with the emotions or feelings attributed to them. This signature can be likened to a beacon that emits a signal identifying its frequency.

A thought of gratitude, for instance, creates a positive signature that will seek out a positive frequency to attach itself to. Frequencies are waves of energy that flow at varying levels of vibration. Just as a positive magnet will repel a negative one, the same occurs with the forces of vibrational energy. Negative energy will attract to a negative vibrational frequency, whereas positive energy will attract to a positive vibrational frequency.

Every breath, every thought, every action creates vibrational energy that intercepts and interacts with the field that proceeds it, thus altering its energy pattern, causing a ripple of change. It's a case of cause and effect. A common concept of this occurrence is termed "the Butterfly Effect," whereby a minute localised change in a complex system can have massive repercussions elsewhere. As a butterfly flaps its wings, it causes a change in the field of energy surrounding it which will continue to expand out, causing changes within the vibrational flow until its power is depleted.

The thoughts, emotions, and acts of every man at every point of his existence contribute to the harmony or disharmony within these channels of frequency. We, therefore, are responsible and obligated to take command, having dominion over them to ensure they flow with and not against the stream of euphony that is, when stripped bare, pure love.

2.5   Love Is at The Core

Humanity constitutes the fullness of universal love, creative power, and energy. It is a love that is and has always been within you and me—a love so complete, it can dry the tears from weeping eyes, heal a bruised heart, save a lost soul, renew a weary mind, and elevate negative thoughts to ones of pure positivity. It is a love that saved me from the black abyss of internal suffering and permitted me to hear wisdom within the void of silence, peace within the stillness of my spirit, and joy in my heart, being present in the now.

Love is at the core of all things. In the creation of all things, love was present. Love is the intention. Love is the hope. Love is the manifestation. Love is humanity. When man determines to put away his ego self and transcend to the higher consciousness of love that brought him forth into awareness, then and only then can mankind be one and an end to hate be accomplished.

The world in its current state is in crisis. We have forgotten how to love with humility and understanding. When you hate your brother, it's you that you hate. When you kill a living thing, a part of you dies. When you disrespect the earth that is your home, you dishonour yourself. We must, as the supreme species, awaken to the esoteric knowledge of who we are before we find ourselves on a collision course with a less-than-desirable fate.

We all possess that which is required to effect change in our own life and the lives of others if we are willing to seek out that which we truly are, being the fullness of intention and purpose of our design. My objective is to ignite a spark in you that fires up your curiosity and passion for truth—a truth so abundant in its glory and power that your life will undergo a radical transformation that goes beyond your current expectations and perceived limitations.

If you are ready to explore a life of endless possibilities and obtain freedom from your physical state and circumstance, then it would be my greatest honour to share with you the profound understanding that was divinely imparted to me, not through a textbook, spiritual teaching, or religious doctrine but by the spirit. My life! The ultimate journey to conscious awareness and awakening to the creator within.

2.6   Transformation

My transformation from suicidal thinking to success happened in an instant, but it took me a lifetime to accomplish. This was not the kind of success built on wealth, fortune, or popularity, but success that encompassed complete inner peace—a success that could only be achieved when I awoke to the self-realisation that I, consciousness, cannot be affected by anything outside of myself. True success is the measure of freedom obtained through the mindful practice of non-attachment. It is only our ego that makes us believe otherwise. Let me take you back to 1982, when I was seven years old.

CHAPTER 3

REWIND—1982

3.1   When I Was Seven Years Old

At the age of seven, having the ability to comprehend my individuality, I realised I was different. I wasn't like the other kids. I was what you could label as introverted or shy. I spent a lot of time in my own thoughts, contemplating the world around me and looking for answers to questions I did not understand. I wasn't sure who I was or what I should be or how I should act, so I mimicked those around me, my sisters, and girls at school.

They were so confident, and it seemed they didn't have to think about what to say before they said it. They spoke, and everyone listened. However, when I adopted their technique and just spoke whatever was in my mind at the time, for the most part I was ignored, told to shut up, or ridiculed before being left alone, wondering what it was I said that was so offensive to have caused such a negative reaction.

I would stand in the playground day after day, year after year, by myself. I would always be found walking along a twenty-metre concrete garden edge. Head down, sadness etched on my face, I paced back and forth, one foot in front of the other, just praying for the sound of the bell. Hurriedly I retreated to my classroom and the relative safety of my desk. To anyone looking in, I was just like everyone else. My desk was my refuge, the only place at school I felt safe. I wasn't required to interact with other students or make conversation.

However, even at my desk, my anxiety was in overdrive. I was consumed with panic and dread, fearing the next time I would be forced to leave my haven—knowing that when I did, I would be exposed and alone, watching as my classmates gathered with their friends, laughing and giggling as they made their way to the playground. I would trail behind, hoping someone would ask me to play, all the while wishing I was invisible.

Sitting at my desk, I was indistinguishable from my classmates. Should anyone see me, they would not be able to tell that I had no friends or that I was the main reason for the whispers and sniggering that echoed through the classroom every day. But I knew!

I didn't want to feel like this forever, so I started wondering what I could change so they might like me. I tried to see what made them carefree, not having to overthink or rehearse what they said. Why weren't the right words available to me? They just didn't like me, and not having insight into my identity, I started to accept their assessment of my worth.

This was reinforced over the years more and more as I began to question every inner thought, not being convinced of who I was or what I believed. The thoughts I used to have of myself that I believed to be true were altered and eventually replaced by the thoughts and opinions of others. I was so confused, it just became easier for me to go along with their assessment. I didn't have a strong enough opinion of myself or conviction of anything different. As a little girl of just seven, I concluded that I had nothing to say worth listening to, so I decided I would say nothing.

If they didn't like me or want me as a friend, then I would not try anymore. I would not care about their cruel words. I would not wait around to see if they ask me to play. I would decide that I didn't need them so when they rejected me, I could feel that somehow, I had chosen to be alone.

Now, having two beautiful children of my own, my heart aches for my seven-year-old self. There was no one to tell her she was worthy. If I could go back in time, I would find her and whisper in her ear, "You are worthy and special and unique." I would tell her of her inner beauty, and that the only person she needed love and acceptance from was herself.

I was not told those precious words that could have saved me from a lifetime of pain, heartbreak, bad decisions, and loneliness. I had to walk it alone and navigate the endless uncertainty of my purpose in a world I didn't understand with people who couldn't see me. For the best part of my early school years, I was invisible. I craved for someone to notice me. I knew I couldn't speak my truth, as that option had always ended up leaving me with a deep sense of sadness. So what could I do to get anyone to notice that I was lonely, I was feeling sad, and I needed someone to care about me?

Maybe if I showed my pain, expressed my emotion, the girls would see me crying and feel sorry for me! Then, just as they did when the other girls cried, they'd band together in empathy, comforting me and fighting over who was going to be my friend and hold my hand back to class. But my tears didn't cause such a reaction from anyone. I cried for as long as I could before pulling myself together, drawing on some unknown source of strength that somehow had the power to get me through each day. Despite my struggles in life at such a young age, there was never anger in my heart for those who had taken pleasure in seeing me cry.

I didn't wish to seek revenge. I didn't hate them for what they did. My only wish was that they would stop and show me kindness. I never blamed anyone for how I felt. I only ever wanted to understand what I did wrong, what I did to deserve their cruel treatment of me. Why did they not see my heart or acknowledge the pain they caused me? It would take another thirty-five years to figure that out.

3.2   Sticks and Stones May Break My Bones

Children can have twenty people as a constant in their lives during these formative years. Nineteen may instil in them positive affirmations of self-worth, ability, and beauty. But if just one of the twenty speaks into that child's life with suggestions of worthlessness, that is what sticks.

Sticks and stones may break my bones, but names will never hurt me! Great little saying that we tell kids to cease their crying when someone has called them a name. But is there any truth to this?

I didn't believe it as a child, and I don't buy into it now. My mother told me this convenient little sentence every day when I returned home from primary school crying about the names I was called, to make everything all right. I understood that she wanted me to ignore the hurtful words of others and somehow be grateful my bones were still intact.

Knowing that the words didn't break my bones did not offer me any sort of consolation for the pain they caused me. Those words cut like a knife and caused my bones to ache, even if they didn't break. Every word, every snigger made under the breath of my classmates sank deep into my being. They formed my belief system, and once driven deep into my subconscious and written into my paradigm, they remained hidden from my conscious awareness for decades to come. When analysing my own childhood, I started to gain insightful wisdom pertaining to the aspects of my childhood that had greatly impacted my adulthood.

3.3   Compartmentalising Trauma

To cope with the trauma of my youth, my seven-year-old brain developed a way to deal with the threat from my external environment. It simply chose to ignore it—pretend it didn't exist. I kept smiling, making jokes, and acting the clown as a cover-up to the pain that stirred just below the surface of my happy-go-lucky exterior. I was too young to know how to handle these emotions, so I developed a technique by which I would act as if totally unaffected.

I compartmentalised my realities in the recesses of my subconscious mind and chose to never think about them or acknowledge their existence. I created the fake version of myself that appeared to be more amicable and appealing than the real one. This fake version formed the basis of the woman I became but left me with a deep sense of disconnect with my authenticity.

3.4   The Baby Elephant

I'm going to start with a story I heard recently that resonates with me and the reasons I got so lost in life. It goes something like this:

> There was a baby elephant born into the circus. From the moment she could stand, a rope was fastened around her back leg and tied to a stake in the ground.
>
> As the days passed, she tried to go beyond the limitations set by the length of the rope, but no matter how hard she tried, she was always pulled back to within the slackness of her restraint.
>
> Months and months went by, and she continued in her attempts to go beyond and gain her freedom, but at some stage she submitted to her limitations and gave up trying.
>
> Then, after many years, she grew big and strong and was now so powerful she could have easily broken free from that rope and snapped that stake as easily as a man can snap a toothpick. But she did not try because she did not believe she could. She had been programmed as a baby elephant, and her limitations had been set in her subconscious. Even though she now had the capability of acquiring her own freedom, she remained defeated and a captive her entire life.

How many of us have tried something many times, continued to fail, so gave up ever trying again? Since then, you have grown taller, become stronger, and attained skills that could now see you succeed, but you don't even try.

Our only limitations are those which we impose on ourselves. Awaken to the realisation that there are no limitations. No boundaries. No one is holding you back from becoming everything you want to be. Just unwarranted, unsubstantiated, imaginary fear!

We must keep trying, keep pushing through the challenges we face. When we can overcome our self-sabotaging doubts, fears, and limitations, we will achieve a level of success that surpasses our wildest dreams.

This shouldn't be a difficult process if the doubts and fears that are causing blockages in your life have been created through situations occurring in your adult years. However, if you find yourself at a loss as to where these fears and doubts originated, then it is likely they were formed in your early childhood. Just as with that baby elephant in the story, they were deeply programmed into your subconscious before the time you could remember.

You can see how programming in our early, most influential years of life can affect the beliefs that we carry on through to adulthood. These beliefs have the power to hijack our present. How can we ascertain what thoughts and beliefs have been seeded and are the root cause of our current blockages?

Well, it won't be immediately obvious and will require you to meditate on your childhood and recall the words that were spoken about you and the beliefs that were instilled in you about your core personality, your weaknesses, and your strengths. Recall your family environment and your position within it. Were you the oldest child where more was expected of you? Were you the middle child who became invisible once your baby brother or sister was born? Or were you the baby who was always trying to catch up to your older siblings, comparing yourself at every turn?

Maybe you were an only child, a child of adoption, or became a ward of the state, being shuffled from home to home but never knowing what a family is. Our childhood has the most critical impact on who we become.

Give me a child until he is seven and I'll show you the man.

Aristotle

This will make sense to many of you who have children and have delighted in the pure joy of watching them grow and learn through early adolescence. Their minds are like sponges that soak up everything that comes into their relatively tiny world.

As children, we have no filter. Everything we hear and see is absorbed by our subconscious and forms the foundation of our identity. We are not born being able to decide what information we accept or reject, because our survival instinct requires us to learn quickly. The negative aspect of this is that children cannot block out the words that are spoken against them or even distinguish that the words of others are only opinions.

As their perception of self has not yet been established, every negative comment, every discouraging word spoken by a parent or other child in the playground or at school becomes the characterisation they identify with, and this becomes the foundation of their false self. The false self is an artificial persona that people create very early in life to protect themselves from re-experiencing developmental trauma, shock, and stress in close relationships. This false or public self appears polite and well-mannered and puts on a show of being real. Internally, they feel empty, dead, or phony, unable to be spontaneous and alive and to show their true self in any part of their lives.

Children create a false self because they do not have enough emotional and social support to become emotionally and psychologically separate from their parents. This adapted self can be either deflated and co-dependent or inflated and counter-dependent. I take a closer look at the false self versus the ego self in later chapters.

3.5   I Found Jesus!

Shortly following my parents' divorce and our relocation to Sydney, I gave my life to Jesus. When I was just twelve years old and in year eight at school, a friend invited me to a Christian camp for the weekend. I had joined her on a few occasions for Friday night youth group, which was run by her older brother. Her whole family were considered "Jesus freaks," so I was hesitant about going, but I didn't have a reputation to speak of that I needed to uphold, and she was my only friend, so I went.

Over the weekend, we participated in outdoor adventures and then compulsory Bible study with the youth group leaders in the afternoons. This Jesus character was described as the very thing I was looking for in my rather solitary life. For someone still suffering from the emotional scars of rejection, a powerful supernatural friend was just the answer. A true friend. Someone who loved me and accepted me for who I was. Someone who could see my heart and knew me without explanation. Someone who would not judge or condemn me. A safe place of refuge during my lonely and troubled days.

The youth leaders asked me constantly if I wanted to accept this Jesus into my heart. During the first days of camp, I was apprehensive and dismissed their pleas. However, there was a moment when I knew, if they asked me again, I would say yes.

The weekend was coming to an end, and I was hopeful that we would have group prayer and at the end when asked the question, "Would anyone like to give their heart to Jesus?" I was going to say *yes*. I couldn't return home without this guy. I needed him, and my time was running out. I prayed for the first time to God and begged for someone ask me about Jesus, knowing I lacked the courage to seek him out.

Luckily, just after dinner on our final night, the opportunity presented. This time, without hesitation, I accepted Jesus as my saviour and gave my life in dedication and service of his gospel. I was filled with such happiness and could not contain my smile or the love flowing from within me.

My mum was suspicious during the car ride home but thrilled I had enjoyed myself so much. I hadn't been sure if I should tell her about my experience, but I couldn't keep my excitement to myself. I proceeded to tell her about my father in heaven and my lord and saviour, Jesus. I was anxious as I awaited her response, but relieved when she finally said, "I'm happy for you darling, if it makes you happy." And that was that.

In the two years after my spiritual transformation into born-again Christianity, a wall of separation sprang up between my family and me. I would retreat to my bedroom and spend hours and hours reading the Bible from cover to cover, trying to learn from it a sense of self-worth that had been lacking since my birth. The words God used to describe his children became the basis of my identity, which was otherwise hazy at best.

As I matured through adolescence to adulthood, life happened, and my faith fluctuated. My belief in a Christian God failed to sustain me or fill me with a peace that I so longed for. However, I never ceased in my pursuit of it.

My awakening to my true spirituality came about following one major revelation, and that was that I had free will. My martyrdom had caused me to relinquish all claim to goodness within me, such as compassion, empathy, and kindness, giving all credit and glory to God.

When I could finally acknowledge my worth free from compulsion of the Holy Spirit, I could finally appreciate my true significance. This revelation obliterated my faith in Christianity, breaking down the stranglehold it held over me and leading me to question who God really is.

CHAPTER 4

BEYOND THE CONSTRAINTS OF RELIGION

4.1　A New Way of Thinking

Whatever your faith, I hope you read this chapter with an open mind and receive it with the intention that it has been written, in love. It may not be easy, as you may be, as I was, programmed to reject any notion that conflicts with the scripture of your faith, but I implore you to continue.

Breaking free of the constraints of my religion was the turning point in my life that came about just moments prior to my awakening. It was the final blockage that had prevented me in the past from obtaining enlightened realisation. What do I mean by going beyond the constraints of religion? Well, religion, although providing me with God to identify with, also introduced to me the concept of evil, perpetuating great fear in me.

Going beyond the constraints of religion to me means awakening to a deeper understanding of our creator that doesn't fall within the restrictive framework of contemporary religion. That is, that not any one God of man's creation or religion alone holds the key to all understanding and wisdom about the universe, but it is the source of all creation and conscious awareness that is God, experiencing life from the perspective of physical form.

What if, for a minute, you put all your beliefs, faith, and understanding about God to one side and allowed yourself to go beyond the limitations of your belief system. What if you could discover a whole new dimension of spirituality that you never knew existed or delve deeper into your current understanding? As expressed in the previous chapter, I had been a born-again Christian for thirty years, and I am grateful for my faith and having insight into the spiritual dimension of my existence. However, what had stopped me all those years from experiencing true spiritual freedom was my understanding and perception of who God is and who I am through him.

I was the first in my family to have accepted Jesus as my saviour and enter a personal relationship with him. Within a couple of years, my mum and two older sisters accepted Jesus as their saviour also.

My mum has been a pastor now for twenty years and is a published author. Her book *The Source: Abraham's Covenant People* is a study of the integration of the church into the vine of Jewish faith. It has been used by Rabbis and Christian pastors throughout the world to bridge the gap between the two opposing theologies.

Along my Christian walk I have led many people to the Lord and believe I have facilitated them in developing their own personal relationship with their creator. My entire family at the time of writing this book are still very much involved and dedicated to their Christian faith, and I pray that reading my book opens their hearts and minds to a new point of understanding.

It is not my intention or desire to lure anyone away from their current faith but to challenge them to look beyond it by raising questions of who God really is. I do not deny the presence of a creative force greater than myself, as I have felt its presence, seen its glory in the earth's beauty, marvelled at the magnificent architecture of the universe, and delighted in the flawless creation of life itself when I am honoured to witness its birth into the world. However, I can no longer reduce this force to the simplicity of a single word, God.

4.2   My Christian Interpretation of God

My perception of God was flawed, and my interpretation of the Bible itself limited my understanding, not allowing me to harness the full power of my creator and realise the creator within. The Bible represented to me a perfect, holy manual to life, outlining the expectations God had of me. Throughout its pages were parables and fables illustrating how I should conduct myself according to God's commandments. It expressed his great and boundless love for me, which underpinned my worth at times of self-doubt.

I clung to the promise of my salvation through faith in his son, Jesus. I believed that my faith and dedication to mould myself into his image would guarantee me a life full of love, grace, mercy, and joy. I felt the Bible and the living words inscribed on its pages were my life-force and the answers to all the mysteries of the world. It was like a secret that only I knew, setting me apart and holding me high above the turmoil of the world below.

I could walk through this life and not be scarred by the actions of others, by the evildoers and those who chose the secular world and Satan as their master. I was relieved to know that I had chosen the one true God, the one who created the heavens and the earth and all they contained in six days.

I attended church regularly. It felt safe—a place I could call home, with people who represented the true love of a real family. During the times in my life that I ever have doubted the truth of my faith, I felt ashamed and pulled away from God, as the guilt I bore was too great. But like everything in life, after my honeymoon with Jesus faded out and the buzzing and tingling in my head wore off, my eyes were opened to the dark side of the Christian doctrine.

4.3   Fear Tactics

The Bible taught me about the devil and the power he possessed to coerce and deceptively tempt me away from my inheritance in heaven, like he did to Eve, disguised as a serpent in the Garden of Eden. It told me of the war that was being waged in the spiritual realms between angels and demons in a desperate battle for my soul. I was convinced that I, too, must be vigilant in fighting the multitude of demons that would seek to destroy me, tempting me into acts of sin and straight out of the presence of my God.

The Book of Revelations also painted a vivid illustration of the horror that was to befall mankind in the coming end of days. It produced such intense fear, there was a time I took measures to stockpile food and survival equipment. I even considered sourcing firearms and undergoing weapons training as personal protection for my family when the time of civil unrest erupted and martial law came into effect.

Before the rise of the Antichrist would come the onset of tribulation and the decisive battle of Armageddon between Satan and Jesus. These fears were confirmed as I turned on the television and became transfixed by the gruesome atrocities being broadcast into my living room every night. It was easy to accept that the destruction and desolation of the world as I knew it was coming soon, because it matched up with my own interpretation of scripture and prophecy.

This is where our early childhood programming and the continued barrage of information absorbed by our subconscious can have long-lasting repercussions until we can rewind and rewire the belief systems and conditioning that keep us locked into a rigid mindset. It is because the subconscious will seek out information throughout our lives that consolidate its default settings, which were usually established up until the age of seven years.

Through it all, I endeavoured to uphold the commandments contained within the pages of the Bible and did what I could to remain faithful to my God. I exercised control, not allowing myself to entertain alternative ways of thinking, in fear of inciting God to jealousy. I would not seek out other gods or even contemplate any other spiritual teaching. I was vigilant in my endeavour to remain within the protection of God's grace, not venturing into the world where the powers and principalities of darkness reigned.

The problem with this? I never felt at peace. There seemed to lurk around every corner a demon or dark force waiting for an opportunity to take me out. I found it overwhelming and devoid of any joy. It was an uneasiness and unrest in my spirit.

A permanent anxiety developed through my realisation of my predicament. I would have to endure this state of being until my dying days. The fear-based ideology of religion bound me like a slave, striving to uphold its impossible expectations. Its scriptures commanded me to protect my mind from the thousands of demonic spirits hell-bent on depriving me of my inheritance in the kingdom of heaven and eternal life.

I was cautious to never let my mind consider any other doctrine, including the then-popular theory of enlightenment. I believed this to be a false light and deception of the antichrist. If I opened my mind for one minute, demons could gain access to my mind and possess my thoughts, luring me into Hades by cunning means.

4.4   The Devil, the Scapegoat

This thinking was terrifying on one level, but being someone who critically examines every side, I had to flip the coin and look at it from another perspective. You see, the devil also presented as a convenient scapegoat for me—an external force onto which I could transfer all responsibility of my sinful or unrighteous acts. This delivered me back into a victim mentality where I could deceive myself that I was powerless to withstand the seduction of sin. I was then able to exonerate myself from the consequences of my unholy ways.

Satan, the devil, the deceiver, whatever name you accredit him has been the scapegoat for humans' inability to control their immoral inclinations and ignoble desires. What people need is not a fall guy but courage to accept accountability for their own weaknesses. When I was growing up, I remember that if my sister got in trouble with my father, her go-to response would be, "The devil made me do it."

Haven't we all at some stage blamed the evil forces of the world for our own wrongdoing?

4.5   Justifiable Punishment for Sin

Whether following the Bible to the letter of the law or backsliding into a world that was dominated and under the control of evil, I found myself in a perpetual state of guilt, shame, and fear. When fully immersed in my Christian walk, the more I attended church and read the Bible, the more things I found that I was guilty of, leading to demoralising bouts of submission and repentance. This left me feeling shameful and imperfect, not inspiring me to change but, on the contrary, slowing ebbing away my self-esteem.

On the other hand, when walking in the secular world, I was constantly reminded of the fact that I was now a sinner and outside of the covering of God's grace. No matter which side of the fence I was on, I felt ineligible for mercy and grace, undeserving of happiness or peace. Without question, I accepted negative experiences, like sickness, poverty and rejection, as justifiable punishment for my sin. I wholeheartedly felt that my belief in Jesus predestined me to a life of misery, with my final reward for enduring this a mansion in heaven and eternal life.

4.6   Am I God's Faulty Merchandise?

This place of unworthiness led to a deep internal sense of depression. I believed nothing of myself was good, and anything that was good was a gift from God. Every sin I committed as defined in scripture, I took full responsibility for, and every good deed I did, I gave all glory to God. So I was left devoid of an identity that had any value.

This implied in my mind a separation between myself and God. I saw myself as faulty merchandise in the production line of human creation when compared to God. I wondered how I could be so flawed and so lacking when I was created in His image, for he was the Almighty. And there was nothing in me that felt almighty or mighty or even anything containing an ounce of might.

I did not look anything close to an image resembling God, his nature, or his thoughts. It seemed we couldn't possibly be spiritually related, because internally and externally, we didn't have anything in common, no matter how hard I tried to become like him. I didn't seem to share any of God's DNA, and thus I felt an undeniable state of detachment. I couldn't find that stairway to heaven or anything that could elevate me into His dwelling place of peace.

This had dramatic implications on my faith. During times of great need, I immersed myself in every aspect of Christianity. I attended church regularly, read the Bible daily, and committed myself to frequent prayer and worship, whilst sharing the gospel with others when opportunity presented. The reconnection to my faith during the difficult times throughout my life did offer me some level of relief and comfort, although it never provided any measurable freedom from my perpetual state of confusion and the absence of a love I so craved.

4.7   Back and Forth from Conviction to Anarchist

I frequently traversed on my spiritual journey from firm conviction in Christ to atheist, to agnostic, as my prayers went unanswered and the healing I sought remained unobtainable. I felt at times in a hopeless pursuit of unfeigned fellowship with my creator that for the most part seemed out of reach.

When I had derived all the good from one end of the faith scale, I found myself conveniently sliding abruptly back to the opposing one. When living at the atheist side of the scale, I could exist in society with the carefree abandon of a child, bankrupt of any regard for right or wrong. My faith fluctuated often to atheist side as Christianity failed to sustain my ever-increasing need for answers and sustainable joy.

Without effort, I would relinquish all responsibility to social correctness, rebelling against the pointless rules and laws society imposed. I revelled in the opportunity to act without forethought or remorse; to be cheerful and unperturbed again, relishing the high energy of drugs and alcohol. I declared resistance to the dominant and oppressive archetype of my religion and revolted against the rigid cultural constraints. For a time, I could erase all memory of God and his unrealised promises from my mind. I found a measure of happiness in this life of assumed ignorance.

I thought, *To hell with God. He hasn't intervened in my life or shown any regard for my heartfelt prayer. He hasn't provided me any assistance in resolving my problems. He hasn't seen fit to heal my body or emotional pain. He didn't bestow upon me a quantifiable portion of mercy or grace as far as I could deduce.* But in fact, my devotion to Him was oppressive and suffocating the life-force out of me. Being in a state of ignorant bliss, I could go about my life without the uncomfortable feeling of overwhelming guilt that was otherwise a constant.

However, the highs I achieved from either end of the faith scale never lasted long before I came crashing down. The higher I got, the harder and further I fell. When I hit rock bottom, the pain was intense, manifesting in me from every angle. Physically, I was a mess; mentally, I was psychotic; and spiritually, I was barren. Maybe religion wasn't the answer, but living without faith in something greater than myself left me lacking motivation or purpose. Once exposed to the spiritual nature of the universe, it was impossible for me to ignore its existence.

I would just have to keep looking for the answer elsewhere. I believed with every fibre of my being that there was more. Religion and the secular world of sex, drugs, and a self-seeking attitude couldn't possibly be the only choices available to me. I was looking for door number three.

Coming also from a strong Jewish bloodline of the Cohens and Levis, being the high priests and rabbis of the Jewish faith, presented another array of variable aspects to my faith that further contributed to my lack of a singular spiritual identity. There was a key, though, that would unlock more meaning to my life and more understanding of my innermost desire for truth. I searched desperately as if in the fight for my life, which I was, to find a concrete, unquestionable, undeniable, unwavering, pragmatic solution to my spiritual and psychological quandary.

4.8   The Trouble with the Word *God*

My trouble was that even the word *God* had so many implications and conflicting meanings, to so many different cultures who all believe their god is the one true God. How is it possible that so many different races of people from hundreds of diverse cultures all have such immense faith that theirs is the one true God, and all others are false?

Have you ever stopped to think that when they pray, they also experience supernatural occurrences? Do they not also receive levels of enlightenment and instruction from their God? All these different religions with their multitude of Gods are honouring the prayers of their disciples while proclaiming to be the one true God.

In every religion, all acts of worship or spiritual discipline are backed by extreme levels of faith—faith that a positive manifestation or answer to prayer will be evidenced in the life of those who vehemently adhere to and uphold the commandments and requirements of their doctrine. So therefore, if you remove the word *God* and go beyond the constraints of individualistic spiritual interpretation, are we not all just praying to the universe with faith that our dreams and desires will be fulfilled? Just contemplate this theory for a second.

If your God is the only one, then who or what is the source of power being leveraged by the children of other faiths? Do not people of faith outside your own also receive blessings, answered prayer, enlightenment, knowledge, understanding, and love from their God? Or does your God not discriminate but honour the prayers of all people, whether Muslim, Hindu, Buddhist, Catholic, or Protestant regardless of the doctrine they confess to uphold? Mankind is the cause of such division and hatred throughout the world in his attempt to define the divine source of creation within the limits of his awareness.

To properly describe God in all absoluteness, you would have to reach far outside the boundaries of humanity's conscious understanding. We pigeonhole God within the pages of doctrine that has been written from the perspective of our interpretation of God's word. Doesn't every father pray for work and sufficient finances to support his family? Pray for the provision of a safe home and food on the table? Doesn't every mother pray for the health and long life happiness of her children? Doesn't every child pray to be loved and accepted? Doesn't every person at the end of the journey pray for a painless crossing over into a peaceful afterlife? Aren't we all human? Don't we all long for the same fundamental rewards of life that are instinctually planted within us from birth?

So why do we cloud this fact with so many labels on what God is? This makes every word ever spoken by God or about God up for continuous debate. Did you know that no two people will have the same interpretation of scripture ever? So then how can we expect a population of 7.6 billion people with over 4,200 religions with any number of Gods ranging from one to 320,000.000 to ever agree with one another when contemplating life's most basic principles?

Therefore, religion will never work and has never worked. It leaves us feeling empty and lacking in any true wisdom or love. However, in saying that, I regard all holy writings of all religions with the deepest respect, as they are and have always been exquisite in their teachings, forming the fundamental principles of life and man's spiritual understanding throughout the centuries. But why the labels? Are they necessary if at the core of all religion is love and peace?

If we can scrap everything else and just embrace the message of love, then peace will naturally follow and all else becomes irrelevant. With love all things can be achieved. I have drawn great revelations from the scriptures, where true wisdom at its very heart is revealed, but sometimes this becomes lost in the story and the characters contained therein, inciting debate over interpretation and causing distraction from its true meaning.

4.9 Good Versus Evil

Wisdom can be found within each of us. Inside, we all carry an understanding of what is good and what is evil, what is wrong and what is right. Occasionally, people do lack this quality, but the majority of mankind has been born able to differentiate between the two.

Why do we then make even the fundamental facts so confusing and conflicting? The world today is changing the very concept of these two most basic truths. Good is declared as bad, and bad declared as good. Should mankind continue to accept good as evil and evil as good, attempting to justify its wrongdoing, then we as a race are headed down a perilous road. My interpretation of the scriptures below may challenge your beliefs on many levels and force you to either cease reading or awaken to the esoteric knowledge that began in the consciousness of man as far back as our ancient beginnings.

The theory of Enlightenment has gathered unstoppable momentum in our present day as the richness of its simplistic nature is revealed. Its creative power is being harnessed by those who desire a life in the flow of non-attachment to the illusionary nature of our perceived reality.

4.10 Who Is God?

In the beginning was the Word, and the Word was with God, and the Word was God.

John 1:1, KJV

This verse suggests that in the beginning was the Word. What word was it referring to, that was with God and was God? If you think of words and the origin of their beginning, you will understand that they derive from the consciousness of God—source consciousness.

Before the word, that is God, could be bought forth, there had to first exist a source of consciousness. It is this conscious creator of all things that gave breath to the word. So then, if we are the creation of God's conscious thought, being made in his image, it is easy to concur that we are an extension of the mind of God and formed out of his very consciousness.

God, being omnipresent, existing in all places, at all times, was a concept I struggled to grasp. Based on my Christian interpretation of scripture, if we were created in the image of God, it made sense to me that God also had the same physical attributes that we were confined to.

However, when you understand that God is not a single entity as portrayed over the centuries sitting on a throne above the firmament of the heavens with the earth as his footstool but a living vibrational energy of conscious thought and creative power that exists in every molecule of our physical and supernatural worlds, you can begin to conceptualise the oneness of all creation that purely exists through our collective conscious thought. Have we projected our own physical representation onto God, not perceiving that the image he referred to as being to His likeness, was not our body but our higher consciousness? We have been created in his conscious image. It is our higher consciousness that reflects the image of God.

I expand on this and its scientific basis in the chapter "The Scientific Theory of Quantum Physics."

The same was in the beginning with God.

John 1:2, KJV

This verse suggests that what was, what is, and what will be are all one and the same, being played out simultaneously without regard for the perception of time. To God, time is eternal and only sustained by the consciousness of human awareness. If the conscious awareness of man was extinguished, then would also the existence of God, as we are God and God is us? And without human consciousness, does God cease to exist?

All things were made by him; and without him was not anything made that was made.

John 1:3, KJV

All creative power in which things came into existence did so from the pure love and the divine nature of creation itself, in which we, being intrinsically one with God, possess and can manifest at will. Our thoughts and conscious existence are what gives form to the physical as we learn how to draw on the universal power of creation and the God within.

We all search for a higher level of understanding and connectedness to God, the Universe, and the power it possesses. When we transcend our lesser self and enter higher consciousness that is where we will find it.

4.11   The Oneness of God

The oneness of God (the source of all creation and consciousness) is for us a concept that defies comprehension from our perception of time and space for which God has no purpose. God is eternal and is the awareness of life itself. No beginning and no end. Through source, all things were created, yet nothing has been created that hasn't always been. For everything that ever was or ever will be has forever existed.

Time is of no consequence, as all that was, is, and will be has always been. The past, the present, and the future all exist concurrently in the eternal realms of the universe. Time is merely a point of awareness in the mind of man that for God is frozen and unchanging.

The clock doesn't tick, the hands of time don't move. Time stands still in the transcendence of immanence. God is nowhere, yet everywhere, existing in no one place yet existing in all places and in all things at the same time. The attempt by mankind to depict God as a human-like being, attributing to him human limitations, does not pay due homage to the absoluteness of who and what God really is. To go beyond the limits of our perception, to conceive of the nonexistence of space and time, relinquish all labels, cross over the boundaries of religious interpretation, then and only then can you glimpse an insight into the supreme divinity of source consciousness and fathom our oneness with it.

It took me a lifetime to find God, yet I always felt God's presence. I am a sub-formation of God experiencing life in physical form. So, in essence, I was always just seeking a connection to my higher self. A moment of enlightenment that provided such clarity I had no doubt. A complete faith that required no effort to achieve sprang up from within me with conviction.

With deep and unquestionable connection to my spirit, the Universe/God was established. The great valley that was a dark void separating me from the creative force of all things had been replaced by an ocean of immense light, colour, vibration, and energy that directly linked my soul to the heart of God.

Every breath I took filled me with a love, peace, and energy so palpable it was the ethereal presence and essence of God literally circulating through every cell of my body. Mankind is not separated from God, as if an entity beyond a spiritual veil in the sky. Mankind is but one expression of God, taking on individual characteristics and experiencing life from varying points of perception and awareness.

The trees, the plants, the animals, the stars, the moon, the oceans, the wind—everything in the universe is a unique expression of God. This is how we are all intricately connected to each other, the earth, and the universe. We are all different manifestations of the one source of all consciousness. God is us and we are God! We have the power to access this creative power at will as our birthright and obligation to enrich the world with our unique understanding.

We are but form, a representation of God. We can utilise the gifts that have been graciously bestowed upon us to reveal divine perfection. There is greatness in us all and the potential to be everything we were designed to be if we can just allow ourselves to believe.

God has been defined in many ways, such as the universe, Mother Nature, vibration, and energy. When you awaken to the power of it, regardless of its title, you will find yourself free from the constraints of religion and open to a truth that goes beyond all that you have believed. You will discover a divine sense of empowerment, gratitude, love, connectedness, worthiness, abundance, and a life overflowing with a joy and happiness that doesn't depend on external circumstance to sustain.

4.12   What Is Eternity?

My only regret is that my journey to this awareness took thirty long years as my soul remained the property of religion—holding the key to the gates of heaven and eternal life in paradise should at my last dying breath I be deemed worthy, yet also holding the key to the fiery pit of Apollyon if found guilty of sin according to its doctrine, sentencing me to eternal damnation. But how can eternity be awarded only at the point of death of our physical body? Eternity has no starting point as defined by its very term. Therefore, we enter eternity from eternity having no beginning and no end.

We have always been eternal, transmuting energy, taking on forms with no regard to time or space. When living out of the physical form without conscious mindfulness, our reality is linear in nature. But when we immerse ourselves in the infinite, we can quantum leap at will, experiencing life in parallel universes, realities, dimensions, times, and space. By connecting to source and using the power of our activated genius and creative force, we can travel within the conduits of electromagnetic waves of energy in which we harmonise with our divine purpose.

4.13   Facing Our Own Demons

We look for anything outside of us to justify our lack of self-discipline over our thoughts and actions. This prevents us from ever evolving, stunting our personal growth and development towards sound moral character.

When we find the boldness required to face our demons head on, we soon realise that they not demons at all but shadows—self-projections of unhealed trauma, fears, and bondages that we have not yet allowed ourselves to acknowledge, process, and let go of. Our demons that we run from are merely fear, conjured up in the mind, holding us captive to the darkest parts of our soul. Once these shadows have been given a safe space to rise to the surface of our awareness, we can acknowledge them, and integrated them into our whole being with compassion and love.

I do not blame or disregard religious doctrine. If interpreted in a positive way, great happiness can be derived from its pages. However, in the hands of the wicked man, it can be a how-to guide to war and conflict. Religion through the ages has been used as a form of control, manipulation, authority, and selfish gain. Mankind tends to take from scripture only that which best lends support to his way of thinking but neglects to acknowledge those passages which convict him of his immoral and corrupt nature.

4.14   Religion Is Not God—God Is Not Religion

Source consciousness is love in its completeness—energy and pure thought that emanates from and within all creation in the known universe. The scriptures contained in the Bible and the ancient writings of the great prophets will remain for me a precious resource of spiritual guidance, and I wholeheartedly believe that these prophets were not only mindful of but teachers of the laws of the universe. I will continue to draw upon and dedicate myself to understanding their spiritual teachings in a new light. I want to share with you the life circumstances that led to my journey of enlightenment and spiritual awakening.

The word enlightenment conjures up the idea of some superhuman accomplishment, and the ego likes to keep it that way, but it is simply your natural state of felt oneness with Being.

Eckhart Tolle

CHAPTER 5

LIVING IN THE MATRIX

5.1 Is Anything Real?

It all started on one perfectly average day in January 2015 when I took a walk to the corner shop. But this day, something was different. Things weren't as they seemed. I could have sworn my eyes were playing tricks on me.

As I looked about at the cars whizzing by, people busily hurrying from here to there, my mind could not process what my eyes were seeing. The world seemed to be out of focus. I had seen the movie *The Matrix* and been curious as to its probability, but now it seemed all too real, as I was experiencing what I thought to be a glitch in the system.

Could I really be living in the matrix? Could my whole existence be virtual reality? This was a theory I welcomed the opportunity to question, as it has been centre stage in popular culture for the past few decades. I had chosen to ignore it in the past due to my Christian faith, but now, seeing what I was seeing, I had to at the very least consider its probability and delve deeper.

The distinct lines of the solid matter I once knew seemed to take on a more distorted, nondefinitive appearance. Everything was a blur. The defined lines of buildings and objects around me seemed to melt into each other, creating the illusion of non-solid matter. It was surreal. Had I just set foot on a movie set? Was I a character in a movie called *My Life*? Was I merely playing my role without being consciously aware of it?

Maybe I was the lead actor in an elaborate experiment, as in *The Truman Show*. I started to question the legitimacy of everything I saw. Was my life and reality merely an illusion? Were the trees and the birds and the wind real or a figment of my mind?

I even wondered about the sky, the sun, and the moon. Were they real or holograms? Was the earth round and spinning at 1,000 kilometres an hour as it hurtled around the sun in outer space at 66,000 kilometres an hour? Was our solar system continuing to expand into an infinite void of space? Or was it flat and stationary? I had lost all ability to perceive what was tangible or what was a hallucination, however real it seemed.

I had a resolute sense of dissonance in my soul and a feeling that I was being played. It was as though I was making choices in my life, but the outcome of these choices had been preprogrammed by someone or something outside of my control. As soon as I gained any traction in my life, something random would occur out of seemingly nowhere to sabotage my progress.

Was life a game? Had I been overlooked when the rule book was handed out? Was this the reason I felt predestined to lose? Did others have the cheat sheet and aces up their sleeves, trumping me on every hand? If so, I needed to learn the tricks of the game and find out the limits of the rules.

I'd had enough of all this inconsistency and now had to take the blinkers from my eyes and enquire about the world in which I was born. My desire for truth about the world was ignited. It became an obsessive quest for informed knowledge and a deeper understanding of the universe and my position in it.

I wanted to know why there were so many wars over land and money. I wanted to know why children were starving in a world so abundant. I wanted to know why my dreams seemed so out of reach. I wanted to know why I was confined to a life that society deemed normal but which I found meaningless. I wanted to know who I was and my purpose in life. I wanted to be free from the prison of my mind's uncertainty.

I wasn't sure where this search would lead me, but once my mind was opened to this train of thinking, I couldn't turn back. I couldn't ignore the ever-increasing urgency to find the answers springing up from within me.

I started researching scientific explanations for this phenomenon. I looked to the theory of quantum physics, but as I believed it to be an opposing doctrine to my faith and the scriptures of the Bible, I didn't accept it as a probable rationale at first. Later, I would come to believe wholeheartedly in this theory. I was determined to find out who was behind this society structure that had me destined to remain a puppet in a show, having no real input into how I lived my life. But be careful what you wish for.

CHAPTER 6

THE RABBIT HOLE OF WORLD CONSPIRACIES

6.1   Who Controls the World?

This is where my quest for truth dove headfirst down the rabbit hole of world conspiracies. How could I foresee that this rabbit hole would lead me into the very depths of my darkest days?

My reality quickly took a disturbing and sinister turn, as I navigated my way through the online rabbit hole of immense evil and corrupt theories. I had only a shallow understanding that I was perhaps in the matrix, being controlled and manipulated by a handful of rich, powerful men who I now identify as the elite one-percenters—those who seek pleasure in conjuring up masterful schemes, subtly enslaving the world, confining the earth's population to a counterfeit reality by suppressing enlightened knowledge, thus retaining all power and control.

These individuals remain behind an invisible veil of powerful corporations and secret societies, covertly initiating various methods of murder to ensure my eventual demise, along with that of a huge percentage of the world's population. Bleak mindset, right?

You will easily see how this progression of thought had devastating effects on my emotional wellbeing. At the time, I was unaware of the implications of this sort of thinking, not realising its impact until it had sent my life on a free fall to the vertical extent of all fear, despair, and anguish.

Ask, and it shall be given you; seek, and ye shall find; knock, and it shall be opened unto you.

Matthew 7:7, KJV

The more I looked for evidence of evil intent by the dark powers of the world, the more evidence I found. I believed that every bit of knowledge I procured was revelation directly from God. He had heard my prayer for understanding and wisdom, finally answering it by opening the door to this rabbit hole.

It seemed as if God had pulled back the cloak from my eyes separating the virtual and spiritual realms and given me eyes to see the truth. I wondered how I had been so blind. The truth was right there in plain sight.

I could now clearly see all the lies that had been filtered into my subconscious mind throughout my life. The news media, music industry, and Hollywood had been subliminally programming my subconscious mind to keep me in fear, keep me locked in a perpetual existence of doom.

I turned on the news each night to see more war, more starving children, more refugees, more natural disasters, more political conflicts, more climate change, more incurable diseases, more biological warfare, more animals becoming extinct, more murder, more hatred, more racism, more political correctness, more chaos, more devastation, more sadness, more hopelessness, more depression, more negativity than a person's soul can bear. And I was somehow confused as to why I felt such negative oppression over my life? Go figure.

I wanted to know who was behind all this propaganda and intentional hijacking of my mind and sense of wellbeing. What was their end game? Maybe it was the antichrist spirit rising, as talked about in scripture? Was this really the onset of Armageddon as so often depicted in the latest Hollywood movies? Was I a part of the last generation of humankind?

Was this a blessing from God, that I was one of the chosen few that would witness the second coming of my Lord and Saviour Jesus Christ? Or was it a curse having to bear witness to the evil that was being brought forth by the antichrist? It was a tough one, but I was leaning towards the latter of the two.

Everywhere I turned, I could see evil, the end of days, the biblical prophecy being played out to the letter. How could scripture be wrong? All things that were prophesied were taking place in this moment in time, in this generation, in my lifetime.

But I didn't want it to be true, so I looked for anything at all to disprove my theory. I didn't want to be part of a world that had forgotten to love. I didn't want to be a citizen of a race that had no compassion for one another. My heart ached every day for those living in the nightmare of war or enduring the unnecessary plight of a slow death through lack of food in a world so plentiful.

Who was behind all these profitable wars? Who was benefiting from the suffering of billions? Was it the Freemasons, the Illuminati, the Jesuits, the Royals, the Vatican, the Rockefellers, the Rothschilds, or some other secret society out to rid the world of the common man? The further down that rabbit hole I travelled, the angrier I became.

Who thought they had the power to decide whether my life was more or less valuable than the next? Isn't all life precious and didn't my life count? Maybe whoever they are can justify genocide on a colossal scale by using science to concur with their belief that the world can't sustain its ever-increasing population. By ridding the world of the weak and unfit they can provide a more enjoyable existence for the few that remain, allowing the earth to replenish itself, thus ensuring the continuation of mankind. Survival of the fittest at play. "Great concept," I hear you say. "Makes sense."

6.2   Global Depopulation—A Moral Dilemma

But there is more to be considered. This theory reminds me of a moral quandary depicted in an episode of *The Good Place*. It's called the trolley experiment, where a trolley or train car is travelling down a track without brakes. Up ahead are five workmen working on the railroad, but there is a switch just before them that will lead the trolley onto another track with only one workman on it. What is the right moral choice in this situation? Well, most people would say change tracks and sacrifice the one workman to save the lives of the five. And I agree that would be the most logical way to approach this moral dilemma.

However, as Chidi, a moral philosophy professor who is a character on the show, found out, there are hundreds more variables that come into play that could have you question your own moral viewpoint. For example, what if the one person on the track is you? What if it is a loved one and the other five people are strangers to you? Wouldn't that scenario see your moral compass spinning out of control? Well, I know mine does when I contemplate this experiment.

It makes sense on many levels that to sacrifice one person to save five is the morally and ethically correct outcome. So perhaps sacrificing billions to save a species might not sound so barbaric. But when it comes to your life, who gets to decide? Who has your life in their hands, and what value is placed on the space you occupy in the world? This is what made me become so frustrated and disillusioned with the powers-that-be whom I firmly believed were there to protect me and my way of life. The idea that they held my life in the palm of their hand, able to extinguish it at any given time for the benefit of the world at large, was outrageous.

Now, I know this may sound like an extreme way of looking at things, but if you have ever seen *The Good Place*, I resonate very much with Chidi. I see a lot of myself in his character. I'm very analytical and find it hard to make decisions, as I overthink everything. I always question the moral and ethical implications that could eventuate from my action or inaction. This can become positively exasperating, as my overthinking for the most part prevents me from acting at all.

After two years of watching every disgusting, evil, depraved, criminal act of those supposedly running the world, I was left feeling sick to my stomach and in a greater state of depression than before.

6.3   The Darkness of Evil Intent

If you go looking for evil, you will find it, and boy, did I! At this point, I just prayed for Jesus to return, as I felt that there was no more hope left in the world. Evil had reared its ugly head and was not going to be stopped until Jesus returned and vindicated all the innocents from the crimes being perpetrated against them.

I mean, I just wanted this life to be over. I couldn't bear to wake up every morning with such a heavy burden of helplessness to change the world tugging down on my soul. Every part of me ached to effect change that would have a significant impact, but I resigned myself that everything that was happening in the world was prophecy, and who was I to mess with that? I just had to have faith that God would take care of things and had all power over the things of this world, heaven and hell. This uncovering of the truth was not of the light but of the darkness and was the precursor to my downward spiral into deep depression and suicidal thoughts—but that's not the end of my story.

I found myself at the end of my three-year search for self-enlightenment and truth in the most baffling turmoil that penetrated every inch of my being. I felt as though I was trapped inside an ominous black cloud of doom and gloom, and once again, I couldn't find my way out. The deeper I ventured down that rabbit hole, the more lost and fearful I became. It was full of the most heinous information, true or not, about the world that had as its only purpose to instil in its readers or listeners more fear and confusion, keeping us so overwhelmed by the enormity of the problem that we are too paralysed by fear to ever act. It keeps us believing we cannot effect change and don't possess weapons powerful enough to come up against such evil intent.

6.4   It's All Virtual Reality

After everything I learnt, the penny finally dropped. I concluded that it's all virtual reality. All of it! I created this virtual state of hopelessness myself and chose to live my life from this place of darkness.

I'm not saying some of the information I exposed wasn't true, but at the end of the day, I haven't witnessed it with my own eyes. I haven't seen any of it. It only became my reality through my TV and computer screen. Once I decided to unplug, it was no longer true and no longer formed part of my day-to-day reality.

You see, what we allow ourselves to become immersed in will inevitably underpin our reality. That's why I say we are not *in* the matrix, but we control it. We decide what we allow to take up space in our conscious thoughts, therefore creating our image of the world in which we live. All these horrible things I had let slowly seep into my subconscious programmed my life to be one that sought and found only evil. No wonder my life went to the dogs so very quickly.

During this time, my marriage faced its biggest challenges. My husband and I were growing apart, as he did not share my desperate need for answers. Our businesses were failing, we lost our family home, and we eventually filed for bankruptcy in early 2017. So much for my high expectations prior to starting this journey. It was anything but what I had envisaged.

This is an example of the way negativity attracts negativity. The reason my life took such a dramatic turn for the worse is because I invited into my life so much negative energy that just attracted more negative energy.

Without possessing the understanding I have now, I never knew that I could have stopped my life from plummeting to rock bottom at any time. I could have woke up one day, arrested all negative thinking, and decided that I was going to start the day on a positive footing, transmuting any negative energy. This would have triggered a vibrational wave of positivity that could have counteracted the negative, therefore halting the effects of my situation. It was time to come off autopilot and take back control of my life.

CHAPTER 7

COMING OFF AUTOPILOT

7.1   Living in the Fog of Denial

As a wife and mother of two young children, running two businesses, I was chasing my tail all day long. Waking from a short-lived medicated sleep, I was immediately struck with a heavy dread and anxiety over the predictable, lacklustre routine of my chaotic schedule.

I was so overwhelmed by the excess of deadlines and responsibilities I would stay awake to the early hours writing lists of tasks that required action. If I failed to write down all the things that needed to be done, they would spiral around in my mind, hence the need for sleep medication. But this left me with a pharmaceutical hangover upon waking that took several Red Bulls and coffees to counteract.

I had an OCD quality to my personality, believing that if I didn't do everything in record time or to my high standard of perfection in every aspect of my life, my world would fall apart. I felt as if I was the glue holding my life and family together. If for one minute I dropped the ball, my life would come crashing down around me.

I wasn't aware of the years passing me by as I became absorbed in the pressures of society to be a superwoman. I was so busy all the time. I looked at my daughter, who was just two-and-a-half years old, and my son, who was nine at the time, and I couldn't remember much of the few years that had gone before. I had become so automatic in my approach to life, I forgot to feel, forgot to emote, forgot to be present in the moment.

I had mentally checked out of my life and was just going through the motions without enjoying anything. My life had become *Groundhog Day*, a repetitive cycle of perpetual dissatisfaction that wouldn't end. I had reached a stage where it was easier just to accept where I was instead of trying to fight my situation anymore. I lost the strength to overpower the constant resistance to change I faced.

After many years of trying to improve my life and marriage, failing to implement the moral and ethical structure I desired, I simply gave up. My counsel was not adhered to, and my advice was not received. I felt obsolete, riding in the back seat without any say in the direction my life was heading.

After thirteen years of marriage, I think I just accepted that this was how it was going to be. My frustration eventually subsided somewhat as my hope diminished and I sank further into the fog of denial. I became a silent partner existing in the background of my marriage. I dutifully carried out the tasks of a good wife and mother, optimistic that I could still maybe inspire the change that I was unable to enforce.

7.2   Where Was My Moral Dessert?

My lack of control within my family life inadvertently caused me to become obsessive in my control of minor areas. I sought perfection in all I did, whether cleaning the house, cooking dinner, my appearance, or anything else that remained within my ability.

This need for perfection was not born from a place of egocentricity but from a place of needing acceptance, acknowledgement, and respect. As I was extremely capable of multitasking and getting things done, people in my life just expected me to sort things out. They came to me with all their problems, whether simple or complex. I was the go-to girl and was always available to everyone.

No matter who it was, if you needed help, I dropped everything and was at your service. It didn't matter if you were family, a friend, or someone I just met: if you asked something of me, I acted without question and in love. I did this with complete trust and an unfounded expectation that my good deed would reap some moral dessert. I see now this was an error of thinking that caused so much disappointment in my life. My expectations of people rewarding me for my devoted service was my downfall, and over the years I had built up an animosity within that I either chose to ignore or was unable to acknowledge.

At my lowest points, when the pressure proved too great and I gave in to exhaustion, I would look to those I had helped, but they were nowhere to be found. My love and kindness grew into silent resentment. All I craved was a mouthpiece to give resonance to my voice and a willing ear to hear. I needed help and didn't know where else to turn.

Not having the courage to stand up for myself or say what I really felt in fear of offending someone, I bottled up my emotions. My nature of wanting to avoid confrontation made it easy for others to overpower me. I would simply retreat from conflict by assuming all responsibility, even though I was not at fault. My perception that I was taking the high road was nothing more than me relinquishing my worth. I let others believe they were right, as I couldn't be bothered justifying myself any longer. However, as the years went on, their truth about me became my truth, and my true identity became obscured.

This conflicting state of being caused feelings of revolt within. I didn't want to be me. In fact, I couldn't stand being me and at times wished there was a way I could free myself from myself, just for a minute, to experience what it felt like to be *normal*. Although I knew resentment was growing within, I didn't know how to hate and continued to let people take advantage of me—hate being an emotion I only aimed at myself. All I wanted was to love and be loved.

7.3   The Plight of a Hopeless Romantic and Dreamer

I was in love with love. I wanted love, wanted to give love and dreamt of a world where only love existed. As a girl of ten, my favourite artists were Whitney Houston, Air Supply, Barbara Streisand, Don McLean, and Lionel Richie. I would listen to them on my Walkman, convinced that when I grew up, I was going to find a love as overpowering as those expressed in the songs' lyrics.

I wanted an all-consuming love that would allow me to reveal the unsurmountable love within me without fear, without hesitation, knowing it would be openly received and reciprocated. I was a hopeless dreamer and romantic who refused to accept that love on a global scale was unachievable. I tried to live within a self-made bubble of rainbows and unicorns even when my life was a mess, not trusting anyone with the turmoil within.

As the years wore on, my capacity to regain a positive disposition after heartbreak became harder to achieve. I identified with the song "Vincent" by Don McLean. I thought somehow my life would end in a similar tragedy. Obviously, I always held out hope for a less tragic end, but as the years of being misunderstood continued and the suffering of unrealised visions and dreams of my youth was prolonged, I came to empathise with the woe he endured and thought that maybe death was the only release from a world content to overlook those who don't conform to society's cookie-cutter image.

Not to blow my own trumpet, but I didn't think this world was meant for one as beautiful as me, and I'm not speaking of my external appearance. I'm speaking of the beauty that was within me that I found difficult to express to a world not interested in seeing it. We tend to only look at the outward expression of others' disconnection from the world, our false self, and fail to take time to engage with others on a deeper level. They didn't see the purity of my heart or the depths of my love for all living things or know the dreams and visions I harboured of a world without hate or conflict. They didn't enquire of my profound aspirations to actively change the world to one I could be proud of. I wanted to see my love for others and the world reflected back to me, to not feel isolated in my dreams of something better but to feel a sense of belonging.

Where were my fellow visionaries who shared my worldview? Where were those who didn't step on others to elevate themselves? Where were those who sought just beauty and dared to expect honesty from their fellow man, those whose eyes could see beyond the hatred, those who dedicated their lives to imparting their talents and gifts to the world, leaving it more enriched by their existence so as not to be forgotten in the archived pages of history.

I continued to serve others, but with the expectation of something in return. When my expectations were not met, a deeply seeded sense of indignation began to well up within. Why am I always putting others' needs before my own. What about me? Why were my aspirations for success and happiness not nourished and tended to but instead ignored as if inconsequential?

7.4   Where Is Everyone?

I longed for someone to support my dreams and desires for a better life, a better world. Excuse me for being corny, but I wanted someone to be "the wind beneath my wings" for a little while. I needed some space to breathe for just a moment to replenish my strength and regain some traction in my life. But every meaningless task or chore was dumped in my lap, never allowing me the time to enjoy my life or fulfil my own dreams. I became a servant, devoid of any respect or recognition.

No one reached out to me or offered me that support. No matter how much I asked, begged, cried, or shouted, no one seemed to notice. I was very private about my family life and never wanted to betray the confidentiality between husband and wife. Never airing our dirty laundry was my custom. From the outside, my life was believed to be the opposite of what it was.

The few times I was in distress and reached out to my family, the tables were immediately turned on me, and regardless of what I told them to the contrary, they refused to hear my truth. I'd withdraw and become silent, not daring to voice my thoughts or become vulnerable, opening myself to further judgement and condemnation. Now it seemed I was designated to sit in the back seat of even my family relationships.

No one even cared to try to contemplate the truth of my reality. There was a part of me that said, "To hell with them! I don't care what anyone thinks!" But there was a deeper need planted in my youth that required the approval of others. I wanted to be seen for who I really was and to be understood. This need for a voice and approval had run me into the ground, where I felt physically, emotionally, and spiritually spent.

I had lived my life, not perfectly, but upholding a strict standard of moral conduct, keeping as much as possible to the commandments of my faith, paying my bills on time and keeping within the framework of society's rigid laws. But it didn't matter. All these things I had become so anal about were just trivial accomplishments at best. There was no unseen benefactor of my good conduct issuing accolades to soothe my painfully burnt ego. Nothing I did seemed to have any effect on those around me. I felt like a victim of my environment, a prisoner trapped in my own reality.

However, have you heard the saying, *the straw that broke the camel's back*? Well, that was where I was at. I knew if one more person said or did one more thing, even if simply forgetting to say thank you, it was going to be the breaking point, sending my feigned cool, happy, and calm persona into one of all outrage.

I couldn't shove one more emotion down. I couldn't accept one more insult to my intelligence, one more false accusation or cruel word to strike my already battered psyche. But what power did I have to free myself from my reality if my freedom relied on the complete metamorphosis of others?

7.5   If You Will Change, My Life Will Be Perfect!

Family, friends, work colleagues, random strangers—they would all have to undergo a total overhaul of their personalities. They'd have to become a new improved version of themselves, incorporating all the character traits and moral conduct I required, for the sole purpose of placating my sensitive emotional skin and expectations.

Anyone who was in my life would have to act in strict accordance with my standards. Now, if this was to happen, I believed my life would be perfect. If everyone else could just change, I could be happy.

Yeah right! Like that was ever going to happen. But believe it or not, I attempted this very thing. I requested, asked, begged, pleaded, tried to inspire change in others to improve my own life experience, but my pleas fell on deaf ears—in hindsight, not surprisingly so. Not an inkling of improvement was gained by all my efforts. Funny that; everyone was quite happy with who they were and had no intention of changing for me. I had finally to come to terms with the fact that this was a hopeless venture and would never be achievable, based on past attempts.

If I couldn't change other people, my other option was to change my environment. Maybe a new house, new town, new state, or new country would be the solution to my unhappiness? Nope. That wasn't the answer either. But I did give this option a fair go before throwing in the towel. I moved home or relocated interstate whenever my current geographical position failed to reconcile my inner conflict. This only compounded my feelings of unfulfillment.

Our family relocated interstate four times over four years, travelled to many different countries, hoping each one might be the place that we could truly call home and feel home. I wanted to feel at peace, no longer thinking the grass was greener elsewhere; to be grateful in that moment, that place where we were, appreciating our blessings before they were all lost.

All the moving failed to satisfy me for any extended period. It was just another city, another house. Different faces but fundamentally the same people. I was running here and there, sometimes of my own choosing, other times not. The disappointment after each move when

I realised it was a mistake was soul-destroying, but to my credit, I got right back on the horse.

I made the best of the situation, quickly falling back into a structured routine of mindless monotony. This I endured until the boredom and frustration became so great they caused me physical illness and depression. I had to do something. The problem was, the only thing I knew how to do was move. I refused to acknowledge the elephant in my mind suggesting the change I required was me.

So again, we up and left for another spot on the map that held the deceptive lure of a better life—a life that my husband and I had skilfully conjured up in our imagination to justify our every move. Even though moving had not provided the happiness I had envisaged, this did not deter me from my endless pursuit of it. Nothing could divert me from my single-minded search for this feeling. I would devise a new plan, a new adventure, another escapade.

I wouldn't accept failure—not where my happiness and the happiness of my family was concerned. I refused to give up, even when true happiness became more difficult to believe in than Santa Claus. This search was a full-time occupation. I was obsessed, and nothing would stop me until I found something of substance that could contribute a depth of meaning to my life that I had otherwise failed to find. I would continue chasing happiness, despite my failures and errors in judgement. I'd rather fail than accept that happiness is just an illusion and no more than a childhood fairy tale.

But I knew I had to stop moving. I had to stabilise my family and devise a new strategy going forward. I had to take responsibility and accountability for my actions. Yes, I was a sweet, kind person who got dealt a rough hand more often than not. Maybe I did feel misunderstood and unappreciated. But were all my negative experiences a consequence of only that which was outside of my own control? Did I not have any responsibility in the shape my life was taking? Was I just a pawn in this game of chess? Was I a victim of circumstance or the mastermind behind it all? Either way, I had to stop pretending all was OK. I had to acknowledge that change wasn't attainable while waiting for an external force to elevate me out of my pitiful state.

7.6   Liberate Yourself

I had to stop living with a defeatist mindset and resolve to liberate myself from this condition of conscious hopelessness. I'd been protecting it, as if it was a beloved friend or a treasured asset. It was toxic, only serving as a reliable source of justification for my self-pity and lack of discipline over my thoughts and emotions.

My life had become nothing more than a burnt, sunken, dry, tasteless cake whose ingredients had been tossed in at will, without a forethought of their bitter flavour and unpalatable aftertaste. Instead of the sweet smell of vanilla bean representing the harmonising flow of what my life should have been, it bore the stench of ignorance and anarchy that was baked into my existence.

I retreated from society and resolved to disassociate myself from everyone to avoid the possibility of a minute situation triggering a volcano of emotional pain, erupting with a force so powerful that the destruction would be on a massive scale, with any chance of regaining myself unlikely. If I had to walk the road alone, it was my road to walk. I was ready to take the first step.

7.7   Pulling the Plug on Social Media

But how was I going to remove myself from society and retreat from family and friendships without causing suspicion? I needed to think of a way to subtly retreat. Sadly, it wasn't as hard as I imagined. I simply stopped posting, writing comments, or liking pictures on Facebook. When I did, I heard from no one. It was that easy to be erased from the thoughts of friends and family. Out of sight, out of mind. When my name no longer showed up in the newsfeed, I no longer existed.

No one picked up the phone. No one came to visit. It was as if I had dropped off the face of the earth. I genuinely wasn't angry, as this was the disconnection I sought; I was just sad that our society had changed our very nature. Social media had become the only avenue in which people could relate and where friendships were sustained, where your number of Facebook friends determined your place of importance in the world. Early on, Facebook was a way for me to justify my life and find approval, but it became empty and provided no true value.

The face-to-face relationships I needed and found some comfort in no longer existed. Technology had robbed everyone of time, and we as a species had lost the ability to be able to relate face-to-face. On the internet, you can be whoever you want to be, and portray whatever it is you want people to know about you. But face-to-face, you can't hide. You can't pretend. You can't deceive. You must be you, and if your social media profile is not accurate, the facade of your perfect life will come crashing down, and others might see the truth of who you really are.

Maybe you're not as happy in your relationship as you've implied. Maybe the happy family portrait that you posted, inscribed with "I love my family," is not a true representation of what is going on behind closed doors. Maybe your life is in ruins, you filed for divorce, or you're drowning in debt after your last summer holiday in Europe. It's funny that we have no problem posting pictures that capture the great moments in our life, but we omit what is really in our hearts.

When I viewed my Facebook profile, I was somewhat impressed by what I saw: a great life, loving husband, beautiful children, overseas travel, friends, and family. Judging only from that, my life was a glowing success. I then looked at my friends' profiles, knowing first-hand the problems they were facing, but even their profiles suggested a perfect life. I decided I couldn't live a lie anymore, pretending to be someone I'm not by creating an image for myself to divert the possibility of any judgement, when all along I was being judged on the fake version of myself anyway.

I stopped expecting, stopped needing, and stopped opening my heart to people. I became fake. Or was I already fake? It was difficult to distinguish anymore. Either way, it was exactly what I detested in others and the only way to avoid having to justify myself and defend my identity, which at that point was undefined and in dispute. I lost faith in people. I lost faith in myself. I hid all my unresolved feelings and sealed up my heart, never wanting to expose a weakness that could be taken advantage of in my already fragile state.

7.8   Time to Get Real

It's exhausting trying to maintain a fake image of yourself just to avoid conflict, but I did it all the time. Plastering a smile on my face, I went about my everyday life, fighting back the urge to scream. I went out of my way to be liked by those I detested—holding back feelings so as not to offend anyone and to maintain my humble, good-girl image. But I finally found the courage to be real, even if it was not a very good version of myself.

Throwing all caution to the wind, I opened that can of worms I'd been so terrified of. I lifted the lid off my emotional vault, not fully comprehending the repercussions of such unbridled expression. If I was angry, you heard about it. If I was upset, you were going to hear me cry. If I didn't like you, I was going to tell you. No more pretending to be happy all the time. The mask had come off, and all forty years of pent-up emotions came flooding out.

Unfortunately, I had no clear direction or focus, just a chaotic expression of all the pain, hurt, and disappointment I had buried for so long. A midlife crisis, you could say! The facade had been dropped and the mask put away. It was now just me, in the raw. No bullshit, no hiding, no pretending. Just me.

My perception of self was shattered, like tiny fragments of a broken mirror that once reflected my image, my ego self. There lay the ruins of my identity, represented as a pile of shattered glass. Was anything of the pile salvageable? Could I painstakingly glue it back together, or did I need to start from scratch? If the mask I had worn all my life was not me, then who the hell was I? What was I to do now with all these emotions? How was I going to make sense of them and find a way to live my life with this unsurmountable negative energy coursing through every fibre of my being?

I decided I had to set myself on a path of self-discovery. I had to shut out all those who had been major contributors to the negative energy in my life. I'd delve into my past to find out what it was that I truly believed about myself and my purpose in this world. Where did I fit in? Who was I?

After tearing down all the protective walls I had built up, dropping all the facades, and getting rid of all the different masks, how much of what was left was really even me? Was there anything of value left that I could use as a foundation for the construction of the new me, or was the remnant of myself merely a vague identity that had been formed from environmental and societal programming throughout my life?

CHAPTER 8

THE EGO VERSUS THE TRUE SELF

8.1   Who Are You?

What comes to mind when you ponder the question *Who am I?* Or when someone asks, "Who are you?" What is your initial thought? You may have been asked this during a job interview or when just simply updating your bio on Facebook, but what do you say when asked the dreaded question: *Who are you?*

You may think this is simple enough. You may believe it's easy to depict a core representation of who you are. But are your thoughts about who you are based on your ego or your true self? Most of who we think we are is derived from the ego and based on external elements of our identity. Anxiety stems from this question as our ego and our true self wage war within. There is a constant struggle for dominance—two opposing selves fighting for their place in our conscious awareness. Our true self is always trying to emerge from the complexities of our ego.

8.2   The Ego

If only your master is an incarnation of God, then who are you? Any kind of exclusivity is identification with form, and identification with form means ego, no matter how well disguised.

Eckhart Tolle, *The Power of Now*

The ego is created by the mind and identifies with the mind and emotion. Only when you can separate yourself from the ego's endless pursuit of want and need can you be present, mindful, and in oneness with being.

The ego is programmed with our default responses to life. When confronted with a situation that is similar in nature to something we have experienced in the past, our response will be triggered automatically as we continue to live unconsciously in the ego. Our default programming will cause us to react involuntarily, without awareness. Only when we become mindful of the ego can we intercede and derail its destructive influence.

This is the biggest issue you will have with your ego. It will keep you on autopilot and make you apathetic to your life. Most of our ego was programmed during childhood. This caused our emotional responses to life to be stunted in their development and to remain generally at an immature level. They are usually exaggerated and for the most part extremely inappropriate in relation to a situation.

During your life, you would have been able to update or rewrite some of your negative programming with thoughtful, deliberate, and critical self-analysis. However, the programming that occurred outside your recollection remains deeply ingrained in your subconscious. Until you have the courage required to actively seek out that programming of your youth that still causes you unnecessary suffering, you will be unable to consciously change it.

The ego operates under the assumption that it is separate from everyone else and disconnected from the world. The ego believes in separation and individuality because it exists only as a creation of your mind, unseen by the rest of the world. It's not to say that all your behavioural patterns and automatic responses are the result of the ego, as many of them are essential to life, allowing us to breathe, move, eat, digest, walk, talk, read, and drive without giving them our full conscious attention.

These automated patterns started developing as soon as you were capable of absorbing information in the womb and your brain started creating new neurological pathways. But they are not ego structures if we don't identify with them, take them personally, or believe they are us. At the time we were born, our conscious awareness was undeveloped and basic in its ability to conventionalise the world outside of ourselves.

As we grew and gained knowledge of the world, we subconsciously fashioned a mental image of how we assumed things to be in the real world. The more information we accepted as truth about our external world, the more complex our inner-world model became.

In time, this world view developed into a meticulously detailed virtual representation of reality. The virtual reality our mind constructed of the world, although bearing a close resemblance to the real world, was always seen through a filter comprising our beliefs and distorted by our misinterpretation. Our interactions with other people also helped to develop our own concept of self, which we annexed to our identity. The concept of self that formed our individuality also created our sense of separation from others.

Our true self does not identify with separation of individuality but sees itself as connected to all humanity, life, and the universe. At an early age, we had a sense of the two distinct sides of ourselves. One is the false mental concept of our ego, and the other is our yet unacknowledged true self. These versions of our self, conflict and at times throughout our life we would interchange them depending on where we happened to be.

As children, we couldn't distinguish between the two. Most people in our life interacted primarily with our ego or false self, not giving due recognition to our inner being, and therefore it was our ego that received continuous validation and was the one we naturally adapted to and felt most comfortable identifying with. This is because the ego self prefers to attach itself only to those characterisations that puff it up, regardless of whether they are based in reality.

Our true self therefore gets forced onto the shelf, being only internally acknowledged during times of personal reflection in our life or when we found ourselves on a path of personal development and self-awareness.

When we are not seen for who we truly are, our ego takes the dominant position in our life, committing us to a fake representation of self and an unreal existence. Our ego and our true self exist simultaneously, at times competing for our attention, causing conflict within, though this conflict is for the most part undetected by others. It can have you feeling at an impasse, not knowing which side of yourself to confer with.

When this happens, it causes a diminished state of identity, destabilising our conviction of who we are. When trying to express our true self, we will come up against opposition and resistance by those who have already established a relationship with our ego. This is the *you* people feel most comfortable interacting with. Trying to comprehend or engage with your true self without awareness of their own true self is near on impossible. Only when we connect with our true self can we see the true self of others.

When we don't have a firm grasp of who we really are, we become anxious, trying to find ways to justify our false sense of self by looking for outside influences to blame. If we fail to find sufficient relief from our internal conflict by blaming the external elements of our world, we retreat to the peace and safety of our true self. This is the one that has, since childhood, acted as a psychological buffer to the real world by allowing us to compartmentalise any confusing, distressing, or traumatic situations that are beyond the ability of our ego to process.

It permits us to view the otherwise ugly parts of our reality with rose-coloured glasses, giving us the ability to interact in the real world while being somehow detached from it. It distorts our reality, becoming something more appealing than it is. We could use it to protect ourselves from the harsh realities of the real world and shield ourselves against the effects of people's negative behaviour towards us. It provides us a mental and emotional escape in which we find refuge for our soul in times of trouble.

Over time, as our ego is validated and confirmed by others, it becomes the self with which we associate our identity. We lose our connection with our true self, blinding us to objective reality and forgetting who we truly are: consciousness.

8.3   Manifestations of the Ego

Aside from providing a worldly identity to live by, the ego lavishes us with alleged confidence, protects us from pain of perceived failure by setting limitations, convinces us of our righteous opinions, safeguards our pride by justifying our actions, reassures us as it endorses our faith, encourages us as we proclaim our truth, and humbles us as we are propelled into social competitiveness. Or does it? Can we successfully live without or put aside our ego? Let's analyse the manifestations of the ego in more depth.

8.3.1   Provider of Worldly Identity

Our worldly identity is the one that has been changing and evolving since early childhood. It began to emerge when, as toddlers, we looked in the mirror and recognised our individual self. At this time, our sense of separation arose, and we began to compare ourselves with others. We were able to recognise the differences in people, whether old or young, skinny or fat, tall or short.

The ability to acknowledge these differences in others also triggered our awareness of our own differences. This formed our need for acceptance or to fit in—the birth of the ego. It is our false identity built upon aspects of our physicality, personality, and beliefs. These include identifications such as name, gender, nationality, religious and political persuasion, height, weight, sexual preference, intelligence, and skills, all of which are non-permanent attributes. Being non-permanent and subject to change, they do not constitute or correctly describe our true self.

These superficial characterisations are not who we truly are and do not represent any percentage of our real identity. The ego's worldly identity of you is so fragile it remains in a constant fight for survival. It is built on a non-solid foundation of subjective characterisations that must be repeatedly validated to be maintained. When not validated, cracks will appear in its volatile outer shell, threatening complete breakdown of its flimsy construction.

This is when the ego goes into battle, defending itself against all opposition by puffing itself up in terms of grandeur and importance. Your ego has a primary goal of self-preservation and will stop at nothing to come to the defence of its base representation of form.

8.3.2   Lavisher of Alleged Confidence

The ego will have you bloated with alleged confidence. This is to say that the ego itself is a false representation of your talents, knowledge, and appearance based on the comparison of others. It is narcissistic and arrogant in nature, only able to uphold confidence whilst engaging in the judgement, criticism, and condemnation of others.

How confident are you in the presence of genius? How confident are you in the presence of physical beauty? Confidence is subjective to those to whom we compare ourselves. When you are compared to someone you believe to be your lesser, your confidence soars, yet in the presence of someone you consider your better, your confidence is at an all-time low. This is the fragile state of the ego. It gives you confidence that is conditional upon your environment and the company you keep.

Therefore, we tend to disassociate ourselves from people we consider our betters so as not to expose our own alleged inadequacies. It is not sustainable whilst based on external factors rather than the internal truth of who we are, not separate but oneness with all. In the absence of comparison, pride cannot exist.

8.3.3   Protector from Pain

The ego hails itself as our protector from pain, but it has a vested interest in keeping us in bondage to pain and suffering. It uses our fear of pain, suffering, or disappointment to keep us locked into a safe way of living. When fearful, we tend to remain safe, not subjecting ourselves to situations that may cause us harm and at the same time delighting in it. This is a failsafe of the ego. When it is allowed to dictate our life, we are prevented from ever reaching our true potential out of fear of failure and unworthiness.

We listen to the ego as it whispers in our ear, *You are not good enough. You are not strong enough. You are not fast enough. You are not smart enough.* This voice becomes our comfort zone, the distinct boundary of our limitations. However, these limitations imposed on us are nothing more than the ego's avoidance of pain. We go to all lengths to avoid pain instead of just letting what is, be. Buddha describes enlightenment as "the end to suffering." Once you embrace pain and suffering as part of life and cease in your efforts to dispel it, you have reached enlightenment.

We can only experience pain and suffering if the pain and suffering has an effect upon our state of being. If a response or reaction to the feeling of pain is no different to a feeling of joy, then what power does pain wield? Only the power we allow it. A sound indifference and acceptance of pain voids its power.

If you seek pleasure, you're avoiding pain. If the ego believes it's here to avoid pain, it continues to thrive.

8.3.4   Convincer of Your Righteous Opinions

Opinions are just that: opinions. Your ego, however, will have you convinced that your opinions are righteous and true above all others. It will have you believe that your understanding, wisdom, and knowledge are superior and not to be debated. If questioned or opposed, your ego will jump into the ring, fiercely defending its position.

An opinion you embraced, maybe in early childhood, and consistently sought validation and support for throughout your life now gives you an indisputable confidence in its correctness. But the problem is, the ego only sought out validation for the opinion that was already seeded, thus disregarding all others. It only sought to add to and deepen the righteous nature of the opinion it first attached itself to, never allowing the growth or development of any other.

This is the way people tend to make or break relationships solely on opinions. If someone doesn't share a similar opinion to you, it is better to end the relationship, as your ego will have you believe that the other person is wrong, incorrect, or uneducated, once again leading you to a place of separateness, judgement, and superiority.

Opinions are other aspects of the ego that multiply and grow in number, forming a large chunk of your false identity. But like all components of the ego, they are not permanent and will change, shifting throughout your life. The ego will have you fight for your opinions, but they are merely a self-gratifying facet of your false self-image. It is imperative that a man's life *not* be fraught with the harvest fruits of his lustful escapades and selfish gains, seeking only to serve his narcissistic, self-absorbed, self-gratifying, individualistic, egocentric self.

When people get taken over by the ego to such an extent, there is nothing else in their mind except the ego. They can no longer feel or sense their humanity—what they share with other human beings, or even with other life forms on the planet. They are so identified with concepts in their minds that other human beings become concepts as well.

Eckhart Tolle, *The Power of Now*

8.3.5 Safeguarder of Your Pride

Pride is a fabricated position of self-importance that is also an illusion stemming from the ego's manufactured image of self. Therefore, the ego has a bad name and people tend to associate it with pride and arrogance. It feels unstable and vulnerable. It understands that it is merely an identity created by the mind and, in an act of survival, will defend itself. If attacked, it will use various protective measures and coping mechanisms to ensure its preservation.

It never wants to be exposed for what it really is, which is not real at all. A lot of our mental and physical energy is exerted in sustaining the ego's belief systems and core values, pride being one of them. To be prideful, you must first see yourself as better than. Pride can only exist in the lack of oneness. To be proud, you must first elevate yourself above another, thus solidifying your sense of separation.

This false perception of separation ignites in us a fear and a feeling that we must protect and defend ourselves psychologically. Much of the ego's programming is associated with shielding us and securing our position. It does this by going on the counterattack should anyone dare question it or its beliefs. The ego will back you up and use your past hurts and injustices to pardon you of any wrongdoing in the now. It will make you feel justified in your anger. It will make you feel righteous in your judgements. It will make you feel blameless in your transgressions. It will make you feel justified in your hate.

The ego will encourage you to experience negative emotions, which it feeds on to fuel its resolve. If you keep ignoring the ego, failing to consciously observe its patterns and influence over your life, it will forever keep you in servitude to its selfish needs. You will remain a puppet, with the ego as the puppet master.

8.3.6 Endorser of Your Faith

Your ego will endorse and support your faith, provided it feeds the ego's need for acceptance, approval, forgiveness, and redemption. Your ego doesn't like being tainted with the unpopular character assessment of malevolent or immoral. It needs to remain inflated with positive affiliations of its greatness, self-righteousness, and salvation. It can then live uninhibited, without the unwanted burden of guilt or denunciation.

The ego welcomes your faith in an external divinity, a supreme being you can transfer all weakness and shameful deeds upon, freeing the ego from the consequences of your actions. Your ego will support your faith for as long as it provides a haven and refuge from pain or unwelcome adverse feelings. The ego will stop at nothing to avoid undesirable emotions, thoughts, and feelings.

8.3.7 Proclaimer of Your Truth

The ego is all about being heard and understood. It seeks validation from everyone it encounters, oblivious to the fact that it is seeking such validation from other egos, all with equal need for a voice. Therefore, most relationships you enter will remain, not by choice, superficial in nature.

It is a naïve expectation that deeper, more intimate relationships could be achieved with the ego dominating your interactions. The ego is teeming with ideas, beliefs, theories, preconceptions, and prejudices that will fight for dominance when confronted with another ego that is just as opinionated. This interaction between your ego and that of another is what creates or abruptly ends potential relationships.

When living solely through my ego, I operated out of my pre-constructed image of who I believed myself to be. This was the quiet, supposedly empathetic, self-claimed humble, self-righteous, validation-seeking good girl I portrayed. I felt entitled in my role as saviour to the lost.

My pride was bolstered as I became the servant of others, fixing their problems and saving them from themselves. I kept giving without expectation, becoming the incurable victim. I was living in self-denial, refusing to take accountability for my own issues, blaming others for what I was responsible for.

I wasn't entirely to blame. It was my ego that lacked awareness of my authentic self and pushed aside my insecurities, too afraid to bring them into the light. My ego kept me so busy trying to validate its rightful position that I failed to realise I was seeking validation for its illusionary sense of self and not for my true self. My true self required no validation.

8.3.8   Keeper of Your Humility

The ego keeps us grounded in humility as it subtly provokes us into social competitiveness. While actively trying to compete in the power-hungry, image-obsessed arena of the 21st century, our humility has no option but to take root. The ego will have you looking sideways as you strive to achieve, making you aware of your inadequacies in comparison to your peers or social circles. It will have you trying to keep up with the Joneses in an endless plight of obtainment of possessions, wealth, and beauty.

This struggle to remain relevant will humble you, leaving you with a feeling of lack and need. External things that the ego deems important do not constitute who you are. They are fleeting, non-sustainable, perishable aspects of the false self.

As long as the egoic mind is running your life, you cannot truly be at ease; you cannot be at peace or fulfilled except for brief intervals when you obtained what you wanted, when a craving has just been fulfilled. Since the ego is a derived sense of self, it needs to identify with external things. It needs to be both defended and fed constantly. The most common ego identifications have to do with possessions, the work you do, social status and recognition, knowledge and education physical appearance, special abilities, relationships, person and family history, belief systems, and often political, nationalistic, racial, religious, and other collective identifications. None of these is you.

Eckhart Tolle, *The Power of Now*

8.4   The True Self

What has been there to witness everything that has happened in your life? What never changes? What is the most fundamental core of who we are? Consciousness.

Consciousness is the fabric of all things. In fact, even science has shown that everything at its core is energy, vibrating at different levels and frequencies. In our human experience, presence, consciousness, or spirit manifests itself as the energy that composes every form.

It is hard to really put a word to this experience, as language is so limited. The easiest way to experience this presence that is you, and always has been you, is through meditation. Meditation, or quieting the mind, helps you to become simply aware of your thoughts and the space beneath those thoughts. That space is You.

It can be said that we are spiritual beings linked to the one source consciousness, all experiencing the physical world through unique and differentiating points of awareness. Our mind controls our thoughts, beliefs, and perception. Our heart controls our centre of love, emotions, and dreams. Our body is responsible for our instincts, impulses, and actions.

A large percentage of who we are consists of our beliefs, thoughts, emotions, desires, and things that we deem important to function in our day-to-day life, but these are not permanent attributes. They are continually subject to change and evolving throughout our life.

Looking back over our life, we see that only one thing has remained a constant: life is always happening right now. Our awareness is the common thread linking our early childhood memories to our present-day reality. Our awareness has been a witness to every event in our life, in a continuous series of present moments. When we delve deeper into our field of awareness, we recognise our qualities, attributes, characteristics, and sense of identity, which more closely describes our true self than merely our personality. This is the essence of who we truly are.

One of the functions of the true self is to direct our life. It interacts with the world by guiding our thoughts by our mind, our emotions by our heart, and our actions by our body. Awareness is our experience of life. Our soul is the field of awareness in which we experience it.

Few of us are aware of this underlying objective that profoundly shapes our approach to life because it dwells deep within us, at the very core of our being. Most of us avoid going into the depths of our being because we don't want to stir up our repressed hurts, fears, and inadequacies. We generally like to keep our awareness at the periphery of our being, just as we generally like to keep our conversations and relationships on a superficial level where no harm can be done.

Unless we become self-aware or enlightened, we are asleep to our true nature. We have not yet come into the understanding of our true self. We live out of a self-constructed centre of consciousness, which is known as the ego.

CHAPTER 9

BECOMING THE BEST VERSION OF YOURSELF

9.1   Are You the Best You Can Be?

Are you the best version of you? Do you look at yourself and your relationships and think the person you currently are is the best version of yourself? I hope you said no, because if we think we are the best version of ourselves, then we stop desiring to become more. We cease to evolve and become stagnant in our self-development.

We should never stop trying to improve ourselves until the day we die, because every day brings forth opportunities to learn and grow. If we do not remain open to and even seek out these opportunities, they will pass us by, and we may often miss the change we required to move on to the next phase of our life.

When we begin to realise our true self and awaken to our full potential, then we begin to dream again. Until we find the courage it takes to turn the mirror back on ourselves and stop looking for outward excuses for our weaknesses, we will fail to reach true awareness.

No one and nothing can change you, only you. When you look in the mirror, is the person staring back at you the person you want to be? Does the image match up with what you want, or does your reflection only serve as a reminder of your failures, evoking a feeling of self-hatred? This is not what we want to see reflected at us. We want to be able to look through any perceived imperfections and see the beauty that is within, our true self.

To do this, we need to critically examine our innermost fears, insecurities, worth, and value. We must first find the courage to pull back the layers, knock down every wall, take off the mask, and drop every facade we have ever invented for ourselves. These have become our Achilles heel. They have prevented us from ever knowing who we are and have restricted others from truly knowing the essence of our soul.

9.2   Dropping All Masks and Facades

There are many reasons we put on these masks, but it's mostly out of fear: fear of rejection, fear of judgement, fear of being unaccepted, and fear of being deemed worthless. This behaviour can also be identified as the ego not wanting to justify itself.

The different facades we use are like different hats we wear depending on the occasion. We may have one for work, one for church, one for our family, and another for our friends. Sometimes we have different ones for each friendship group contingent on that group's expectation of who we are, based on their first impression. If you befriended a person at the pub on a night out and partied all night long together, that becomes the person you are to them and the impression that will no doubt remain during the lifetime of your friendship.

But who are you at church? Do you take that same version of yourself to church on Sunday, or do you put on your church hat? Do you dress and carry yourself differently at church than you do when socialising? I'm sure the answer is yes! We like to conform to those around us so as not to be singled out. We don't want to be perceived as the only one with problems when those in the pews next to us seem so spiritually blissful. But you shouldn't worry, because they are not. They also put on their church hats before leaving the house.

It doesn't matter what hat people choose to wear, because underneath, we are the same. We have all been cut from the same cloth and possess the same indistinguishable attributes that make us human.

9.3   The World's Youth, Obsessed with Self-Image

It saddens me when I see the world's youth immersing themselves in themselves, taking thousands of selfies in every light, from every angle, with different filters to capture that one image—that one image that looks nothing like them! The one they share with the world more closely resembles the artificial, pretentious, clone-like creatures plastered all over the internet, after Photoshopping the already distorted unrealistic image.

Why do kids as young as six years old feel uncomfortable in their own skin? Why are they not content with their physical appearance? At this tender age, they are already beginning to feel the pressures of a society gone mad, an imperfect world looking for perfection, making us strive for unrealistic images of self-worth.

It is not normal that kids are transforming their external appearance to remain relevant in a world so fake it's hard to see the forest through the trees. They are hiding their beauty behind layers of makeup, fake eyelashes, fake hair, and fake lips, so scared that anyone might see their true beauty, which requires no enhancement or cosmetic effects, no camera trickery or angle persuasion, just them, naked-faced, pure and fresh, having the love of self so great, they are comfortable in their own skin and don't require accolades and tongue-in-cheek compliments from relative strangers.

What has happened to our society that we find it almost impossible to be genuine? I'm no saint. I've had my fair share of procedures trying to appear younger, sexier, thinner, and more beautiful. But for whom? I can delude myself and say I did it for myself, but even I know that's a lie. Was it for the random strangers that pass me by at the grocery store, believing me worthy enough for a second glance? Did this fulfil my need for acceptance?

No, it didn't. The acceptance I sought had to come from within—a humble love and acceptance of myself that wasn't reliant on the approval of others. A deep love for our fellow man will only come when we first find deep, pure, and true love for ourselves, all of ourselves.

9.4   Love Your Body—All of It!

Loving the goods bits is easy; it's learning to love the bits that don't appeal to the perfection-obsessed pages of the glossy magazines that is challenging. Appreciate every wrinkle, every dimple, every scar, every freckle, every pimple, every hair on your head (or lack thereof). This is the unique vehicle that was given you and the only one you will ever get. It is an extraordinary vessel that takes care of you every day, ensuring your heartbeats, oxygenating your blood, ridding your body of toxins, and keeping you alive every day so you can live a life worthy of it. Respect it and love it, because it sure does love you despite your cruel and punishing treatment.

Just don't obsess over it. It is the physical vessel and comprises only a small percentage of your fullness of being, and yet you give it 100 per cent of your time, energy, and focus, dedicating your life to ensuring its perfection and all the while neglecting the largest portion of you that matters. The real you.

9.5   Let the Real You Shine

The real you is the one who one no one else sees, the one who only exists in your thoughts, the one who is more beautiful than you can imagine, though never permitted expression. It's the one who connects with the world, the one who loves, the one who inspires, the one who dreams, the one who has visions, the one who imagines a world that doesn't hate, the one who wants to make a difference, the one who wants to achieve great things, the one who wants to inspire others to greatness, the one who hungers for an opportunity to be heard, to be seen, to emerge from the dark recesses of your soul and come into the light and just shine.

Will you let your true self shine? Can you let it be known and acknowledged by the world instead of shunned to the outskirts of your everyday life, never knowing what you could become? Don't you regard this side of yourself? Do you offer any respect for its wants and desires? Will your ego continue to take centre stage, or will you recast the lead role in your life with the real preforming artist, with the Universe as your supporting act? The Universe favours our true self and will do everything to ensure its growth and development to awareness.

Don't get caught up in the external pressures of society's unreal expectations. Just be the best darn you that you can be. You are worth it, and if you continue to exist in this lesser, superficial version of yourself, you will never be happy, never experience true relationships, and never experience true love, because people won't be loving you; they will be loving the image you created.

Take off the mask and be the real you. Encompass all that you are, all that is unseen. Each person who has ever lived has experienced moments of self-doubt, fear, and confusion. You are no exception. You, and you only, know what it feels like to walk in your shoes.

Self-doubt, fear, and confusion are natural emotions and should not be shoved down and never acknowledged. Address these emotions, study them, analyse them, get to know their causes and their effects. Don't allow them to stop you from doing that which you want; use them as your inspiration and motivation, and then muster the courage to let them go.

9.6 Your Authentic Self

Until others have endured your pain and counted your tears, they will not understand the source of your fears. You know your pain, but you also know your strength. Be not concerned with the opinion of others, only your opinion of yourself.

There is no performing artist in this world who you should idolise and put on a higher pedestal than yourself. You are your biggest and sometimes only fan. If you don't believe in yourself enough to reserve front-row seats to your own show, who will? You are likely to have hundreds of varying versions of yourself that you interchange throughout the day, depending on who you are with or where you are. This leads to a place of diminishing identity where your true self gets diluted over time and you end up with a washed out, undefinable image of who you are.

Let's imagine you can do away with every incomplete version of yourself, which are all operating at a fraction of their potential, and pour all your energy into one spectacular version of yourself. Imagine being comfortable enough in your own skin that you can be you always, with all people. You'll never have to invent new ways to hide all those things about yourself you never want to see the light of day.

You can't hide them, no matter how hard you try. There is always going to be someone or something that knows your trigger and exactly which button to push. You may have people in your life who confront you and challenge you, knowing just the words to say to make you lose your grip on the mask and expose that which you were trying so desperately to hide. And when they do, you find yourself in fight or flight mode, scrambling for ways to not let the fragile wall of your outward persona crumble.

9.7   Fight or Flight Mode

In an act of self-preservation, our ego goes into defensive mode and immediately on the attack at the very thought of someone getting too close—close enough to see through our disguise. And if we start to lose control of the situation, feeling the lid lifted on our emotions, we run! We run as if a lion is at our heels. The idea of exposing any vulnerability sends us into a state of panic and anxiety.

At this point, adrenaline is released by the truckload in a bid for survival. What is it that makes us do this? Why are we so scared to be genuine? Is it that we are shrouded in a thick cloud of shame and guilt for the things we have done or haven't done? Or is it that we don't know how to be anything else? We don't know what lies beneath the mask.

Have you at times trusted someone enough to let down your guard and take off your mask, only to be judged and have your vulnerability used against you? This can force us back to immediately donning the mask again, pushing down the pain and emotions of our true self, not finding a safe place in which to express it.

I have spent most of my life like this—not having a soft place to fall or let my voice be heard without having to endure the disparagement of others and without anyone providing me with sound guidance and instruction on how to change. Only when I had exhausted all my external options of assistance and reached a place of absolute numbness, not wanting to die but looking for one good reason to live, did I finally turn my focus back on myself.

9.8   The Scars We Bear Reveal Our Strength

This was a turning point in my life. Although most of my life was spent in self-examination and discovery, there were many forces at play that blocked my path to total freedom. Most of these existed because even though I dissected my life back from childhood and continuously sought the truth of my authenticity, I only ever focused on my destructive negative attitudes, beliefs, weaknesses, and inabilities.

Until just recently, the most important aspect that escaped my insight was my strength. I neglected to examine and give focus to that which made me unique—the qualities that made me a one-of-a-kind creation. When I could finally stop obsessing over everything I didn't have, all the people who had disappointed me, all my failures, all my regrets, all the judgement and criticism, then I could make way for seeing the wonderful qualities I possess.

First, I needed to find my centre, my true north. My compass had been spiralling out of control for too long, and it needed to stop. I had to dig deep and find the love in me, for me. No one and nothing was able to fill that longing for love and acceptance.

Should I dare to ever expect it, I had the belief that I would once again be left with a deep sense of disappointment. I knew if I wanted to feel loved, if I wanted to feel worthy, accepted, and happy, I could no longer look to my husband, my kids, my family, my friends, or my circumstances. It had to start with me!

I began to reject any negative thoughts I had about myself and started to assess all the qualities I possessed that were good and worthy of love. I went back to when I was just five years old, before the voices of others permeated my beliefs. I recalled the memories and even got out some old pictures. What I saw was the opposite of what I had become. I saw a little girl who was so full of life.

I was extremely funny, witty, and engaging as a young child. I was always smiling and having fun wherever I could find it. My heart was full of love for life. I had a love for nature and for animals, and I remember I would always try to swerve my bicycle around the ants on the footpath, not wanting to kill any one of them lest I divide a family unit.

I would find baby birds that had fallen from their nests and nurse them back to health. I was an old soul in a little body who wanted to know the answers to questions I didn't understand. I remember being just five years old and lying outside on the trampoline. I would look up into the sky and wonder how big its expanse was. I wondered how far space continued and if you could ever reach its limits.

I was a dreamer and spent a lot of my time alone and in my own thoughts. Those around me thought I was introverted and shy, but I wasn't. I was just thoughtful and introspective at a very young age. I was very creative. I was analytical and questioned everything. I was kind and compassionate and empathetic. I was a deep thinker and never looked at the small things but had the ability to envisage the big picture.

How then, when at just five years old I possessed all these amazing qualities, did I wind up with a self-defeating personality? I was well equipped to achieve remarkable things.

As I continued to mature from the age of five through to early adolescence and then into adulthood, the qualities that had once defined my true nature were replaced with doubt and false perceptions of myself. Where did that sweet, loving little girl go? I really liked her and wanted to find her again. And I did! I'm so grateful she is back in my life, and that after the longest time, I acknowledged her existence. I was not forcing her to just exist in the recesses of my memory but allowed her to be free and live as she had always dreamed.

Don't we all want that? To give ourselves permission to be childlike? That means not worrying about the accusing stares of others and instead letting our enthusiasm for life and our childlike joy overflow and permeate every aspect of our existence. Not that during my life these intrinsic qualities did not surface, because they were always with me. However, they failed to be validated by me or others, so they quickly lost all the energy required to maintain them, dissolving into the darkness. Our weaknesses are our greatest strengths, because it's only in our weakness that our strength is manifest.

Our scars show that we have been in battle and come out victors. With the right focused energy, people should feel you coming. They will not only recognise your beauty but seek it out. Any physical scars you bear become invisible when the energy that resides in your true self goes out into the world before you, searching out a compatible frequency to the one you're on. It's not out of your reach.

If you are still breathing, there is still time. Be brave and let go. Reach far and wide into your memory, and there, waiting for you, is you in your most authentic form. This little child holds the key to your true happiness. If you are just willing to reach out your hand and allow him/her to take his/her rightful place in the present, you will no longer have to hide. You will discover a freedom you never thought possible.

9.9   Resistance to Change

As we grow and effect change for the better, we may come up against resistance from those closest to us, who may reject the changes we wish to make and try to keep us exactly as we are.

Have you ever gone on a diet, wanting to improve your health and feel more confident, only to find, for example, your partner bringing you home a box of chocolates or Chinese takeaway, knowing you are trying to lose weight and are going to find it hard to resist? Your loved ones don't do this because they intentionally want to hurt you; most likely, they are subconsciously trying to sabotage your progress. Why would they want to sabotage your efforts to lose weight and become healthier? Because even though you're looking sexier and being healthier could appeal to their egocentric side, there is another side to your change that they do not feel comfortable with.

If a woman loses weight, starts to feel more confident, fits into those skinny jeans, and has more energy, it could have a negative effect on her spouse. It could cause him to become suspicious of the motivation for her change. It could cause him to become jealous when she leaves the house, even if just to go to the local shops to get milk and bread. It could make his security about his own appearance come into question. It could make him feel he is not good enough for her anymore. Or the changes she has made for herself might make him feel pressured to enact change within himself. This is very common scenario and can in some cases be the reason relationships and marriages fall apart.

If you are the only one in your relationship who is constantly growing, developing, maturing, and in pursuit of the best version of yourself, and your partner has not evolved past a certain age or time in your relationship, a void will begin to develop, and you will eventually outgrow your spouse. This is the resistance we come up against when wanting to change. It can come from a spouse, a parent, or a child who is not only content in seeing you remain exactly as you are but who will pull out all stops to ensure it. Your changing affects their life too and will require them to change, which may not be something they are ready for or even desire.

Don't let others' selfish needs keep you locked into a substandard version of yourself, when you know you can be better and do better. This is your life, and you only get one of them, that we know of, so don't you owe it to yourself to be the best damn you there is? If friends or family don't support the changes you are making, you must decide to go it alone. Decide that no one and nothing is going to hold you back any longer from becoming the best version of yourself.

CHAPTER 10

ADDICTION

10.1   My Personal Journey into Addiction

I was what you would call a high-functioning addict. Before I go on, I think it pays to mention that during my years of self-discovery, I was in and out of my drug addiction, either running on high energy or suffering the consequences of the come-down.

I'm not here to justify my addiction or minimise its destructive nature, but I want to give you an honest insight into why I chose to do drugs. I was not uneducated or stupid or without alternatives. I was an intelligent woman who made an informed decision to do them, though in hindsight not fully understanding the negative repercussions. I made a conscious choice. But why?

10.2   Why I Chose Drugs

At first, they seemed to be an escape ... right up until they became my prison!

You see, I didn't start my addiction ever believing I would become addicted or that anything bad would result from it. That's the deceptive nature of the beast. No one ever starts using drugs without the complete conviction of one's ability to control them. Only when it's too late do we realise our inability to free ourselves from what has now become a physical and psychological dependency.

It all started innocently enough in late 2015 when my husband and I were offered a small quantity of methamphetamines. For the twelve years we had been married, we had not been exposed to this lifestyle and preferred a few drinks with friends on the weekend. But for some reason, that day, my husband accepted his mate's neighbourly gesture and happily received the drug without question.

It didn't seem like a big deal but rather a bit of harmless fun. That day turned out to be one of the best days my husband and I had shared in a very long time. We reconnected, talking for hours, laughing, basking in our renewed love and appreciation for each other, experiencing an intimacy that had been long forgotten in our relationship.

Now, you would have to understand that at this time in my life, I was despondent and lacking any joy or happiness. I was waking up each morning going through the paces of getting kids ready for school, making breakfast, cleaning the house, paying bills, and administering my businesses. Reliving the same repetitive cycle every day had slowly begun to ebb away at my soul, diminishing my once-exuberant passion and enthusiasm for life.

With the drugs, for the first time in a long time, I remembered what it felt like to be happy, connected, and in love. I was pumped about my life and felt on top of the world. My body wasn't aching, I was full of energy, my brain fog had cleared, the headaches that I frequently suffered were miraculously cured, and I instantly started making sky-high plans for my future. Suddenly, I wanted to draw again, and the creative side of my brain just kicked into action.

The drug had literally snapped me out of my life of apathy. It had allowed me to bypass the conflict of my conscious mind, and it became a sort of doorway to my higher consciousness. I felt as if I had transcended the problems of my world, connected with God, and awakened to the world around me. So it's not hard to understand why I wanted to experience this again and stay in the flow of this high-octane energy that, in my delusion, I was convinced was providing me with an abundance of profound truth and enlightenment.

Unfortunately, the time came when the drug failed to produce the same initial euphoric high as before, creating the need for more and more. As this stage, the damage was done. My husband and I were now dependant on it to just function at a normal level, with any expectation of a high being an unrealistic pipe dream. Now we were going from what we perceived as normal to extreme lows very quickly. It wasn't a matter of choice anymore. Our brains' chemistry had been so severely altered that we were unable to experience any level of happiness without drugs. The part of the brain that handled our production of serotonin had been overridden by the drug and therefore ceased to operate naturally when perceiving low serotonin levels.

When we could finally acknowledge that our drug dependency was out of control, my husband and I would quit and go for extended periods—months at a time—without touching them. However, it took just one bad day, and we would deceive ourselves into thinking we could handle just a little bit and then that would be it. Before long, we were sucked back into the cycle, and the process began all over again.

The difficultly in us both being addicted is that when one of us wanted to quit, the other didn't, and vice versa. We were becoming a bad influence on each other's attempts to quit and growing further and further apart as the drug psychosis started to take hold.

So why choose drugs? Why do people do anything that is bad for them? Why do people drink alcohol, knowing they will have to suffer the consequences of a hangover the next day? Why do people eat too much when they know they will get fat? Why do people smoke when they know it causes lung cancer?

Back to my original question: why did I choose drugs? They released me from my dumbed-down apathy and forced me to question why I could not obtain the same level of energy, clarity, and happiness while sober as when I was high. Why did I need a drug to experience these feelings of wellbeing? Why when sober was the meaningless nature of my life without purpose so evident?

The road to my addiction, as devastating as it had been, also forced me to face the underlying issues that caused it in the first place. I was not an addict for the thrill of it, but because it provided a temporary escape from the harsh reality of the world around me.

10.3   Will Power Is for the Undisciplined

Will power is not a personality trait that only a lucky few are afforded. In fact, it doesn't even exist. There is no special power, no magical fairy dust that can stop the addictions and bad habits in our lives. Bad habits are just that: habits.

And though addiction has a chemical dependency, it doesn't mean there is no cure. Both bad habits and addiction are, at their core, no more than the repetition of a single bad choice for prolonged periods of time. Addictions and bad habits will, for some people, be hard to break due to the emotional or social connection attributed to them. If you have ever been a slave to addiction, you will know what I'm talking about. Certain people or places invoke your impulse to entertain a bad habit or addiction.

For instance, the minute I would get in the car, I went for my cigarettes. You would think the car wouldn't start without them, as I literally would not press the ignition button until my packet was in reach. And what about friends? Do you find that most of your circle of friends also share your addiction? That's because you know you won't be judged by your bad decision or need to make any apologies for it. This leaves you feeling comfortable, guilt free, and unashamed.

You can then consciously accept your bad decision as a good one, easily exonerating yourself from any accountability or responsibility. I know this because I have been there and know the hundred and one ways. I used to justify my addiction to myself by saying, "Well, I'm not as bad as those other people. I still get up every morning and look after my kids. I still shower, brush my teeth and take care of my physical appearance. I can give it up anytime. I just need it now to feel happy in this moment."

10.4   Deceptive Self-Justification and Convenient Labels

This self-talk was deceptively cunning at making me believe the lies. I believed them without question, because they agreed with my self-destructive desires. Who wants to believe the truth—that your bad habits are making you sick, that your body is losing its strength, that the high isn't worth the come down?

In that moment, when our thoughts and desires are focused on our addiction of choice, we develop temporary amnesia about the truth and just listen to the deceptive lies we have concocted for ourselves. There is no doubt about the physiological component of addiction, but for the most part, it is habit and lack of self-control.

Most of the time, we don't even realise that we have bad habits, as they have become so deeply seeded in us that we do them without even thinking. I know during my life, my knee-jerk reaction to any distress was to light up a cigarette and pour myself a Jack Daniels. Even though it had the effect of calming my initial anxiety, it was not a sustainable antidote. It could not counteract the poison, the unresolved unhappiness that was still pumping through my veins.

We all self-medicate in one way or another to avoid having to experience unwanted feelings or emotions. But when we continue to self-medicate without addressing the feelings that led to our dependency, we will forever be trapped in the cycle of addiction. What really defines *will power* is "self-control" and "self-discipline." The only reason the term was created was for those who needed an excuse for their lack of both.

If bad habits are a repetition of bad choices conceived by bad thoughts, we must first change our thought pattern. By changing the way in which we handle our emotional response to stressful stimuli, we can start thinking differently, making better decisions, which in time will create good habits. Anything unwanted in your life is within your power to change. As a society, we find so many ways in which to invent new mental illnesses to justify a certain behaviour instead of having the courage to address the underlying cause.

This is again an example of how we like to hang on to our baggage and self-destructive labels, giving ourselves permission to remain in our destructive lifestyle. If we continue to subconsciously give in to our bad habits or addiction and don't consciously probe the grounds for their creation, they will always keep us locked in bondage. No amount of willpower will ever be enough. You have the key, though, and the key is your thoughts backed by positive action.

10.5   Forgive Yourself First, Then Face the Truth

If you are locked in the shame and guilt of your bad habit or addiction, then the first thing you must do is forgive yourself. If you have no one in your life to show you a little empathy or compassion at a time when you need it most, then you must be willing to give it to yourself.

Be gentle with yourself, as only you know what you've been through and the inner demons you have had to fight just to stay alive. But you have, because somewhere in you is a fighter, and you have not thrown in the towel yet. Don't ever think that what you see in the mirror while in your addiction is the end of your story or defines who you are. What you see is only the external manifestation of your internal pain. What will define you is not the weakness it took to get you here but the strength you find to break free.

If you're waiting for someone or something outside of yourself to change, you'll forever be just a passenger in your life, never at the helm. When you admit that your circumstance is due to your own bad decisions, you can acknowledge your role and take responsibility for your part in it. Then change becomes possible.

10.6   A Lifeline in Disguise

I know that during my addiction, my drug of choice represented a lifeline thrown to me in the shallows of my darkest despair, providing me a brief high and escape from the reality of my hopelessness. It was but a fleeting moment in time, maybe long enough to catch my breath and forget about my troubles for a while, before that same lifeline that had saved me from my initial perilous fate dropped me right smack bang into a bigger, wider, deeper, darker existence than that which it had plucked me from.

No matter how bad your situation or emotional state, your addiction or habit is not a Band-Aid solution. There is a better option if you are committed to requiring more of yourself. You might be homeless, broke, estranged from family and friends, and feel your life has become unimportant and the pursuit of anything more is nothing but a futile venture. I'm here to tell you that it's not a dream that is out of your reach, and don't ever stop dreaming.

When we stop dreaming, we stop trying; and when we stop trying, we stop believing; and when we stop believing, that's when all hope is lost. This world would be a sadder place if you remained lost forever. When you take your life back, the drive and determination it will require will surpass that of any who have not found themselves at the end of that dark and lonely road.

It's when we reach a dead end in our life that all the treasure within us is revealed. It's like a pot of gold at the end of a rainbow. It seems impossible to find, and sometimes we must hit rock bottom to find it. When we do, we are well rewarded with the most precious gift of all: a realisation of what hard, tough metal we are made of. In the same way gold is refined, we too must be refined. Only when gold is exposed to extreme temperatures and changes to a molten liquid can the impurities be removed. Sometimes in life, it is only when we go through the fire that the impurities in our life can be eliminated. When we come out the other side, we will be purer.

Your addiction has a silver lining. You can't fall any further, so the only way forward from here is up. You can do it, and you will do it because you know you must do it.

10.7 Do You Know Someone Suffering from Addiction?

Maybe this chapter doesn't relate to you, but you have a friend or family member who is struggling with addiction. If so, then I want to give you a little advice. What they need most of all is your compassion, mercy, and unconditional love. Never stop being that person. I know this may be challenging at times, as addicts are usually so immersed in their own shame and guilt they may isolate themselves from you, not wanting you to see how far they have fallen.

But I can guarantee you, they want you and need you in their life. Their addiction is an outward manifestation of their silent screams for help. You must understand that most addicts did not start their journey in life wanting to be a slave to addiction. They most likely got there when everything they tried continued to fail and they just gave up.

Stay connected by continuing to invite them to family functions and social events. Become a safe place for them to come and unload. Allow them to share their struggles. Don't lecture but listen. The last thing they need is to be told is how bad their addiction is, because they already know. What they are unsure about is their worthiness of your love despite their addiction. Be sure to leave your judgement, condemnation, or condescending stares at the door, as these will have them retreating into their addiction.

All you can do is offer them encouragement and support when they need it—not enabling the addiction but letting them see their true value and worth reflected in your eyes. Treat them with respect and understanding. Don't be the light that shines a spotlight on the very thing they are trying so desperately to hide. They don't ever want you to see them in their weakness or forget who they really are.

10.8 Your Addiction Doesn't Define You

You too have a purpose, and your addiction doesn't define who you are. But it's up to you to take that leap of faith and find out what you are really made of. You will surprise yourself just as I have. To do this, you will have to remove the people in your life who don't support your decision, and there will be many.

A lot of people have gotten comfortable with you as the addict in the family, as you have been the one they could look at to make themselves feel superior. You may have become the scapegoat for all your family's problems. If your friends or family don't support you, then you just have to ride solo for a time until you are strong enough to reintroduce the new and improved version of yourself.

10.9   The Forgotten Addict

Addiction is complex, and it isn't a case of one size fits all. We can't ignore that society has a huge part to play in the worldwide addiction epidemic. We should not expect the addict to bear all the blame. The addict is a by-product of a broken societal structure. Addiction isn't a clear-cut case of an individual's guilt or innocence. It stems from the changes to our society, which has neglected its citizens by failing to provide a way of life that ensures a decent standard of living for all.

We are constantly bombarded on the internet with before and after pictures of crack addicts. With their open wounds covering their once beautiful faces, a few stained teeth left from their once full smile, they pose for yet another mugshot. We frown upon these who are deemed as the garbage of society and watch them on reality TV as they entertain us with their pathetic escapades. But who are these people? What are their names? What caused them to exist in such a despicable reality?

Do you think they come from a wealthy neighbourhood or from affluence or privilege? I think not! These are the ones who society has forgotten about. Did they choose this existence, or were they a product of their environment?

This is not to say that some don't have a choice, but if you are born to parents who are addicts, growing up in a world where drugs are the norm from a young age, then how can the world at large hold you fully accountable? These people you see as the ugly face of drugs are generally bound in poverty and, once addicted, have only the financial resources to buy dirty drugs off the street. They physically and mentality deteriorate at lightning speed. They share a similar plight to that of the mentality ill and homeless, who are also statistics of a broken society, in which the tools for them to transform their lives are not made available.

The government tries to treat the symptoms of drug abuse by providing a synthetic substitute and sending the addict back on the street. But why does it not seek true wisdom as to the cause and acknowledge its responsibility? We are living in a world gone mad where the rich spend tens of thousands on a hotel room for the night while the poor are left hungry and freezing on the steps outside.

What we need more of is love and compassion. We need to inspire, not condemn. We need to uplift, not cast down. We need to accept, not reject. We need to be kind, not cruel. We need to help, not hurt. It starts with us as a society resolving to always remember the forgotten.

10.10   The High-Functioning Addict

Now that we have looked at the obvious, in-your-face side of addiction, I want to turn your attention to the high-class, high-functioning, white-collar addicts. This could be your neighbour who goes to work in a suit and tie every morning, a mum from your kid's school, a teacher, your accountant, your lawyer, a local policeman, a councilman, your hairdresser, members of your congregation, a court judge, a politician, or even you yourself. These are the addicts who are not broadcast in the media. They remain silent in their addiction and prefer to retain and uphold their image of self-control and righteousness.

High-class addicts usually maintain respected occupations and are therefore not judged as harshly as the unemployed living in varying levels of poverty. This category consists of recreational drug users and encompasses other forms of addiction, such as work, gambling, prescription medication, sex, exercise, and pornography, just to name a few.

All forms of addiction have crippling effects on the lives of those who are held captive in their tight grip. Addiction should *never* be measured on a sliding scale of acceptability, because it's not about what is acceptable; it's that we are all human and use addiction as a coping mechanism in most cases as an escape. Addiction is addiction! It has many different faces and should never be perceived as having just one side.

10.11   Social Responsibility

We are all partakers in this thing we call life and all cope in different ways with the trials we face and the pressures of a world on the brink of insanity. No one should ever look down at anyone in judgement but instead show kindness and compassion to those who need a helping hand. Be that hand to pick yourself up if there is no one else there. Be that hand that reaches out in love to lift another in crisis. Don't we all need a helping hand now and then, to be shown a little kindness?

If you are not an addict and have ever battled with addiction in any form, you have my full respect and admiration. You should consider yourself blessed to have never fallen victim to its deceptive appeal and be proud of your strength and ability to refrain.

CHAPTER 11

THE CONFINES OF SOCIETY

11.1   Where Has Our Freedom Gone?

Have you started to sense that the freedom you once had no longer exists? I was born in 1975, and growing up seemed so much less stressful than what the youths of today must navigate.

It seems that in today's society, our choices have diminished, and our way of life is confined to a preset timeline of achievement, with success spelled out for us from the moment we are old enough to comprehend that good grades lead to good jobs, good jobs lead to stable income, and stable income qualifies us to get a mortgage to buy the Australian dream home, get a nice car, and send the kids to college. If you're lucky, healthy, and haven't had to dip into your super during your life, you may be fortunate to have a rest and enjoy a few good years in your old age.

Why is it that besides some minor variables, the above timeline is our only option? Why are we forced to concede to a life pre-planned from the moment we are born? This structure has never sufficed and will never persuade me to accept its mundane, meaningless, and deceptive portrayal of what life should consist of in the pursuit of happiness.

I long for a time when we, as a society, are once again permitted the freedom to make real choices in the lifestyle we wish to lead and the way in which we raise our children.

11.2   Traditional Schooling and Education

Intellect or education cannot be measured solely on a person's ability to recreate, reiterate, or regurgitate information derived from a textbook.

Natalie Preci

If you ask most people how they would describe an education, they immediately refer to schooling and university degrees. But there are other ways in which a person can be educated that don't involve the traditional structure observed in the present day. The schooling system that is implemented throughout the world and that is a compulsory requirement was introduced only two hundred years ago.

So, what about those who lived before this? Were none of them educated? Of course they were. There are many ways in which a person can become educated that doesn't consist of repetitive programming of information derived from a textbook.

Have you ever considered the accuracy of the information being taught in schools today? What is it our kids are really learning? I'm 100 per cent in favour of schooling to teach children the basic mathematical, literacy, and scientific principles that provide the foundation of their education. However, our current schooling is not teaching children how to think critically and independently, encouraging them to explore their creativity and question ideas that don't correspond with their beliefs.

This structured establishment creates another generation of workers and slaves for the big corporations. If just a portion of the curriculum was dedicated to promoting the freedom of individual expression, we would have young adults entering the world with a sense of self and confidence that they can achieve anything they set their mind to, regardless of a common core score on their abilities and intelligence. Some of the greatest minds and entrepreneurs who ever graced this earth never continued their schooling past the ninth grade.

If your passion is to become a doctor, lawyer, or physicist, then yes, schooling is required within the archaic structure. But what percentage of schooling supports the dreamers, the creators, the visionaries, the artists, and the future of inventors?

I address this topic only as it was raised during a recent dinner with my neighbours, who insisted that if I didn't hold a bachelor's degree in math, I was unfit to teach my eleven-year-old son, and that my taking him out of the schooling system for any amount of time was irresponsible and neglectful of his education.

I have removed my children at various times from school so I could expose them to the world through travel to different countries and allow them to experience different cultures. This gives them an appreciation of the country in which they are blessed to be citizens but also teaches them compassion and empathy and instils in them a sense of humanitarian obligation when faced with those less fortunate. I wholeheartedly believe that their exposure to real-world learning has in no way proved to be a deficit but a complement to their social development and ability to cope with real-world situations.

Why is this form of education so restricted and frowned upon as detrimental? That's where I get claustrophobic within the current structure of society. It is tightening its grip on the people to a point where the most fundamental rights of a parent to be able to influence the upbringing of children are gradually being taken over by the state.

The choices that were once available have now been written into laws that are punishable by prison time if not upheld, which is a reality that makes me uneasy. I mean, yes, I live in a democratic country, but where did all our freedoms go?

Have you not noticed little by little the restrictions imposed on you by the state under the guise of being for our own protection? But from what are we being protected? Are not the fear tactics used by the media a strategy through which to impose such restrictions without any opposition? Why have we as a people forgotten to seek out greater experiences in life and become too complacent to even think outside the imposed structure of the societal norm?

11.3 Our Choice or a Product of Our Birthplace?

From the moment of our birth, has not a huge portion of our lives and beliefs already been mapped out for us? If you are born in Italy, there is a good chance you will be raised Catholic. If you are born in Iran, you will most likely be brought up in the Muslim faith. If you are born in Thailand, you will be Buddhist, and in India, Hindu. And in other Western countries. you are likely to believe in some denomination of the Christian faith.

So, what gives us such conviction in our faith which, in all reality, was a product of our birthplace? Is our faith just the programmed belief system of our youth and nothing of our own choosing? Have we just subconsciously been conditioned to our way of thinking by our parents, family, and the society in which we were raised?

But it doesn't end there. If you are born in China, then you are limited to having one child. If that child is a girl, then her fate has in most cases already been sealed. If you were born into the battlefield in Syria, the reality of your world is bleak as you cower in the ruins of a once thriving city, wondering if the next blast from a distant rocket launcher will be the one that ends your existence. What about those babies born in Africa who commence their sorrowful journey to their death from the moment they are brought forth from their mothers' wombs? Are they somehow not as worthy of life as those born into the privilege of Western society?

Would you agree that reality about our life and identity cannot be conclusively defined as one concrete ideal? But all human beings view the world from their own interpretation of their existence in society, whatever that may be.

Some people look at reality as the unchangeable physical world around us. Yet our ideas about reality are deceptive and keep us locked into the restrictions imposed by our physical environment. What if your reality was not subject to what your eyes perceive but was quite pliable and could be moulded and configured in a way that reflected your wants and desires? Reality is not something that is determined and is in fact more consistent with fluid, like the flowing waters of the ocean—an ocean that creates waves of probable reality. I set out on a mission to prove this theory.

CHAPTER 12

WHAT IS REALITY?

Reality is an illusion that only exists in the mind of who perceives it.

Natalie Preci

12.1 Reality Is an Illusion

Is what your eyes perceive real or just a figment of your imagination? Do bad things really happen to you, or have you created them? What if I told you that everything that has happened to you is because of you, because of your expectations, because of your beliefs about what it is you expect to see and experience?

Reality is an illusion and only exists in the mind of the one who perceives it. There is no past and no future. The only time that exists is now. Every passing moment can affect the next, and it is not confined to any set perception of reality. If this is true, then why aren't all of us living our dreams in accordance with what we want? Because what we want isn't backed by conviction of its possibility to manifest into reality.

Our dreams will remain only dreams until we change our thinking. Our thoughts have creative power and unless we become the master of them, they will keep us locked into a substandard reality of our own making.

Only what we truly believe constitutes that which we experience. You may say the sky is blue, but is it? Is it blue? What colour is blue? Do you perceive the colour blue in the same way I do? Maybe, and maybe not. We don't see colour; our brain processes a representation of colour. The retinas in our eyes absorb the light that emits at a frequency, converting it into colour.

You might say that even a child can easily identify the colour blue from other colours, and I agree this is true. But haven't we all been programmed with this information from the time we were born? We were told the sky was blue, and we believed it. Our brain remembered this information and programmed it deep into our subconscious.

12.2   Flat Earth Theory

Another example is the fiercely debated topic of flat earth. Is the earth round or flat? Now, if you ask flat-earthers, there is no doubt in their minds that it is flat, and they will provide limitless proof to back up this theory. I know this topic causes many to arc up, and to this day, I'm confused as to why. It's not a question of who is right or wrong but a concept that should have everyone question its validity and probe the facts. Have you ever considered it? Have you ever really contemplated the notion? Well, I have.

And I can say that for me, one day the earth was round, and the next day it was flat. I could be wrong, as I now realise that everything in my reality is subjective and nothing is what it seems. But let's just say you were willing to consider the theory. You would first have to put aside your existing truth for a moment and give me the opportunity to prove that reality is merely an illusion and that even flat-earthers have a strong argument.

OK, so let's begin. Here are some questions to ponder.

1. If the sun and the moon are visible in our sky at the same point in time, that would suggest that the other hemisphere is left completely devoid of light.
2. When you see the moon in a crescent, you can see the blue sky and clouds behind it. If it's a solid mass, then how can a large portion of it become translucent?
3. If we really are spinning at 1,000 kilometres an hour, how can you go up in a hot air balloon, remain there for any extended period, and come down in the same location?
4. How can the force of gravity explain why we remain fixed to the surface of the earth, yet a feather can float without being subject to the same force?
5. Why can you not see the curvature of the earth no matter how high you go?
6. If planes ascended to 36,000 feet and travelled at the same elevation without dipping the nose of the plane at constant intervals, they would fly right out into space.
7. How can a plane that is travelling at 900 kilometres per hour land on an earth that is rotating at 1,000 kilometres an hour, sometimes in the opposite direction, without noticing the opposing trajectory?
8. Just try to find one real image of our spherical globe earth on the internet. You won't be able to because they don't exist. All images of our earth are digitally made.
9. Search the internet for a direct flight from South Africa to Perth, Australia. It's a straight eight-hour flight, yet all flights divert to Dubai. This is because, on a flat map, Dubai is the logical stop, as it falls directly between the two locations.

These facts are not so much theories as truths that I have witnessed with my own eyes, and they present me with conflicting viewpoints. Because as much proof as there is for flat earth, if I was to believe in it wholeheartedly, I would have to disregard science, which is something I can't do.

I would have to accept that the planets, our ever-expanding universe, science, geography, and history are all fabrications. That man has never been to outer space, and the moon landings were fake. That Antarctica is not a continent but an ice wall holding in the seas. That beyond the ice walls exists land, just as described by Richard Byrd following his expedition in 1963 and prior to the Antarctic being declared a militarised zone.

It's a thought-provoking subject that should help you to see the objectivity of reality. However, as it opens my mind to countless more theories, I choose not to entertain the matter any longer. I resolved to myself that the shape of the earth was inconsequential and decided to see just the beauty, perfection, and divine creation that it is. You see, our eyes will see whatever it is they are programmed to believe, and the power of our subconscious mind will create whatever reality it is we choose.

Reality is whatever your subconscious has been programmed to accept as real. If this programming was done during your early years of life without you knowing it, it remains as your rigid point of awareness of the world in which you live. Your brain will purposefully seek out from your environment the information required to support and compound the beliefs you have. It's only when you can open your eyes and challenge that which you perceive as real that you can fully comprehend the power of your subconscious mind and see the truth that exists in plain sight.

We all have the power to accept or reject other realities that exist concurrently. When you awaken your conscious mind, you can enter the world of infinite probability. When you change your beliefs, they have no option other than to manifest into your reality. The idea that reality is an illusion created by your subconscious mind is supported by the advance in scientific discovery, in the field of quantum physics. The theory of quantum mechanics holds the key to interpreting the new way in which we look at the universe and our connection to it through the one united field of collective consciousness.

12.3   The Scientific Theory of Quantum Physics

The atoms or elementary particles themselves are not real; they form a world of potentialities or possibilities rather than one of things or facts.

Werner Heisenberg

For some people, the idea of trying to wrap their heads around complex theories of physics could have them skipping this chapter and moving on to something less complex, but if you are one of them, I encourage you to keep reading. I am going to try to explain it as best I can in layman's terms, as I don't want to lose you in a whole bunch of scientific mumbo jumbo.

I do not hold a bachelor's degree in physics, nor have I had any formal education on the subject, so my understanding will be based on my extensive research over the last three years. The scientific world and the spiritual community have always been at loggerheads, with neither side being able to conclusively prove or disprove the other's theories.

Physicists rely on mathematical equations and experimental evidence to prove a theory before deeming it fact. When it comes to God, the spiritual nature of our universe, and our own consciousness, scientists and spiritualists have for many decades been at an impasse—until now. To best understand quantum physics, you first must gasp quantum mechanics. I'm going to give you a glimpse into the subatomic world of infinite possibility and limitless potential.

The unseen, subatomic world is all around us, just waiting for us to create or pull into existence the very reality in which we want to live. You are about to discover the power you possess within yourself to design your life, just as an architect designs a building. And even more exciting, you will come to realise that you are not living in the matrix, you are the master of it.

Would you be shocked to learn that you experience the effects of quantum mechanics every moment of every day, as it forms the fundamental nature of our physical world without us ever being aware of it? That's because the quantum realm is a sea of microscopic particles, electrons, protons, and neutrons that are the building blocks of the atom, thus forming all matter in the known universe.

The splitting of the atom was a major scientific milestone. However, since then, through the advancement of scientific technology, scientists have discovered the most amazing phenomenon. They have viewed electrons behaving in the most mysterious way that contradict everything we once perceived as the framework of our reality.

If you could shrink to the size of an atom and observe electrons in this quantum state, you would see that they defy all the laws of space and time. They do not act the same way they do on a larger scale, which is what we see. They behave in an entirely unconventional way. They bounce around with no set point of origin and no clear destination, popping in and out of existence at will and occurring concurrently in more than one place, as if existing in different parallel realities simultaneously.

This is the science that has brought into question the very fabric of our reality and the idea that on a subatomic level, all matter in the universe is not in any one fixed place until it is observed or measured with the expectation of it being there. Therefore, prior to electrons being observed, they are hard to pin down and only exist as waves of probability. But the true nature of electrons and the strange way they conduct themselves still have the science world stumped.

The term *quantum leap* comes from the abnormal way in which an electron, when agitated by light, can jump from one orbital path within the atom to another without traversing the space between the two points. In other words, it kind of time travels within the atom. This means that everything around us and our perception of reality is in fact very similar to the matrix. It is not absolute or predictable and, therefore, can be manipulated and controlled if combined with the power of universal energy and our subconscious mind.

Everything that makes us, makes up the universe, and we are connected in every way to everything. Our consciousness is the only thing in the known universe that doesn't consist of any matter at a particle level or subatomic level and exists independent of our physical self.

Our consciousness therefore must have all creative dominion over the physical world, meaning our thoughts are what force matter into our physical reality. Understanding the fundamentals of quantum mechanics will help you comprehend the creative power we have at our disposal when we learn how to hack the quantum state.

12.4   Reticular Activating System

The information processed by our brain that forms our reality does so with the assistance of a little piece of brain matter located at the base of our brain called the *reticular activating system* (RAS). The RAS is responsible for processing all the information we are exposed to at any given time. Acting as gatekeeper of your conscious mind, it filters in only the information it deems worthy of your attention.

Out of the 2 million or so pieces of information we are exposed to through our senses—such as touch, taste, sight, and hearing—the RAS must make the difficult decision of which bits of information to accept and which to discard. Our brain can process approximately 150 bits of information out of a sea of 2 million. It uses a complex formula and algorithm to make choices the millisecond our brain perceives sensory or visual information. This would be an impossible task for even the most sophisticated computer to handle.

Consider for a minute the challenges the RAS faces. It must remain constantly alert and vigilant in its capacity to help us detect any potential threat or danger to our physical wellbeing while at the same time seeking out information that pertains to our senses and focus. The RAS also controls our sleep patterns, wakes us up, and directs our attention. So, in relation to our senses, when we experience pain associated with illness, disease, or injury and the focus of our attention is concentrated on that part of the body, the RAS will kick into action and look to that area of the body that you are focused on to process the information associated with it.

You would have experienced the power of the RAS at some point of your life when suffering from a headache. As soon as you divert your focus to the pain, the pain somehow increases. That's because the RAS will not only pay attention to that which we focus on but also confirm and compound it. Therefore, when we focus on pain, it tends to amplify.

If you have children, you have seen the way they behave after falling over and scraping a knee. They will scream and cry in such pain, you would think someone is torturing them. However, the second you divert their attention with the promise of an ice cream, suddenly the pain subsides.

This is neuroscience. The RAS controls our reality using our senses and focus. What we focus on or deem important will be the information the RAS will process, ignoring all other 1,999,850 bits available to us at any one given time. If you want to change your reality, change your focus.

CHAPTER 13

SOCIAL ISOLATION

13.1 Global Epidemic

The condition of social isolation is a major factor in the cause of many diseases and not just something experienced by those who are locked up in prison. A large percentage of the population endures the torment of isolation and loneliness in silence. This is an epidemic, and it has been discovered that isolation has astounding implications on not only our psychological wellbeing but also our physical health.

It is our core nature and requirement to function in life within the framework of a diverse social structure. When we are removed from this framework by choice or chance, our brains and bodies start to exhibit physical symptoms of this separation. It can cause conditions such as depression, anxiety, brain fog, fatigue, dementia, and even Alzheimer's.

There is new research that suggests that all these illnesses are not as incurable as the medical field had once believed, and that we can not only reverse their effects but, in some cases, achieve full recovery. This is done by assessing the entire body chemistry on a whole and not just the part that displays the symptom.

As our body and all its parts, including the brain, are a complex network of organisms that are constantly interacting with each other, we must look for the root cause of the symptom first. This can present in a part of the body that would otherwise be considered unrelated to the initial perceived problem. When we are isolated from others, when suffering from depression or helplessness, we can spiral rapidly into suicidal thoughts if left unchecked.

This is a heartbreaking place in which I spent many years of my life, feeling the physical pain of my heart breaking as I wept in silence and with desperation over the extreme loneliness I experienced.

13.2   Open Up the Lines of Communication

This is a disturbing phenomenon where you can be surrounded by thousands of people and still feel utterly alone. This happened to me when I travelled to Las Vegas for a global business conference at the MGM Grand with 25,000 people in attendance. I was there with business acquaintances and friends, and yet I felt so alone. It was one of the most difficult, heart-wrenching times in my life and was the precursor that identified my need for personal development and started me on my journey of self-discovery.

On my return home after being away for ten days, I knew I had to access the underlying cause of my inability to connect with people. Why did I feel this overwhelming sense of loneliness in a crowd of people? In the back of my mind, I knew it was my insecurities. I believed that I masked them well, but the negative energy they created was apparent and clearly evidenced within me. It was something I had attempted so many times in the past to reconcile but with no success.

The thought of having to bring my core issues back to the table for critical analysis initiated intense apprehension. I was convinced there was no cure for my lack of confidence, and I would remain isolated and invisible forever.

Maybe you experience this in your marriage or relationship or within your own family unit. It's as if you are there, but you are not. You speak, yet no one hears you. You feel alienated within your inner circle. Your partner comes home from work and is too tired to talk, and you ask your kids how their day was with only a grunt for a reply.

You're living under the same roof but emotionally disconnected. No one is communicating.

For us to gain the skills required to reach out in support of those suffering in our community, we must first be able to support those within our family. It starts in the home, reaching out from there into our community and then the world.

Our sense of responsibility to assist each other through this journey called life must be heightened to effect real change on a global scale. Too many souls are suffering internally. It manifests itself externally throughout society in the form of depression, suicide, addiction, loneliness, mental disorders, violence, hate, and jealousy. We can stop it if we just take the time to care.

13.3   Technology—Friend or Foe?

Technology has also played a major role in this disconnectedness. It has impacted the dynamics of the family unit over the last few decades, where family dinners have been replaced by the TV, computer, iPad, iPhone, and all forms of visual stimulation that require little spoken communication.

The sounds of voices and laughter have vanished from the family home and are replaced by the sound of televisions blaring from every room. It's time to unplug from this virtual reality and reconnect with those around you. Really get to know what's going on in the hearts of your loved ones.

Don't just ask what they want you to know. We must gently probe to reveal the truth. No one wants one's weakness to be judged, and most of us find it hard to be truly vulnerable. Opening up about things we are ashamed of or don't even understand about ourselves can be challenging. Yet if we really care about improving our relationships, we must give those we love plenty of opportunities to share their innermost struggles, so as not to leave them to overcome their obstacles internally.

Just talking through a problem with someone else will provide relief and often reveal the answers you were searching for. All negative emotions or behaviour stem from a deeper internal fight. Jump in the ring with those you love, take up the fight with them, and help build their self-esteem by giving them an opportunity to voice their concerns.

I understand the challenges in this, as technology has become a babysitter for parents who are working long hours and come home exhausted. It's easy to have your kids sit in front of the TV because once you turn it off, they lack the ability to find things to entertain themselves, as they have become so contented with being entertained.

Until we force our children, through necessity, to tap into the creative centre in their brain, the neuron connectors in their brain will begin to fizzle out, and they will lose the capability to think independently. This will sorely hinder their progress into adulthood and limit their achievement in life.

Boredom is a great tool that inspires creativity. Don't be scared to let your children experience boredom, because this is where the creative forces of necessity are at their peak. You will be amazed at what can be accomplished in that place.

13.4 Emotional Isolation

Isolation falls into two distinct categories: physical and emotional. Emotional isolation held me in bondage for many years due to feelings of being misunderstood. My perception was that I was unappreciated for who I was. When not permitted to express ourselves, we suffer in silence from the frustration and bitterness that develops, and which starts to decay us from within.

During year after year of living in silence, I used to imagine my funeral and everyone standing over my coffin, blaming me for my demise. I heard whispers from the grave that it was my addiction, my weakness, my lack of self-control that caused the disease that eventually took my life. But little did they know, I had already written my own eulogy in a final attempt to put their misconceptions to rest.

I did not die from disease but from the *dis-ease* within my soul. The constant disharmony stemmed from the injustice I was afforded when I had done the very best I could throughout my lifetime to help others despite my afflictions and the challenges of my youth. This emotional isolation was crippling and sent my thoughts contemplating a sad, pitiful end to my life of regret.

Who writes her own eulogy while still living? Only someone like me who could not find a single person who had ears to hear. There was no one to hear the pain and discontentedness that consumed me, and to offer me some compassionate counsel. This is not to say there weren't moments of happiness sprinkled throughout my life, but at my core, I was deeply depressed, as I could not articulate the perplexity of my mind's overwhelming theories of the meaning of life.

My lifelong analytical search for truth and understanding about the fundamental nature of self and society as a whole failed to find a springboard to bounce off. But there was a point when I had to stop waiting for others to acknowledge me and choose to acknowledge my own truth about who I knew I was beneath the outward persona I portrayed. I had to find a platform to have my voice heard. And if you are reading this, I did finally find it! This is me and this is my story. I no longer must wait until my eulogy is read on the day of my funeral to express who I am.

13.5 The Upside of Isolation

Although isolation for some is a terrible predicament, for others it is essential. Some people spend their lives in the company of others in fear of being alone with themselves. If you don't spend much time in your own company, there is a good chance there are things you are trying to avoid having to deal with. When we become isolated, removed from the white noise and distraction of life outside, we can start to quiet our thoughts and find the peace required to achieve personal growth and self-examination.

Without carving out moments in our day when we can just stop what we are doing and remove ourselves from the outside noise, we will fail to hear that inner voice guiding us to self-realisation. We all have that inner voice that whispers to us constantly, reminding us that there are things in our life that need to be acknowledged, changed, or removed, but not ignored. It's in these times that we can really connect with our higher self and gain crucial wisdom and understanding. To spend at least one hour each day in this reflective state will help you to grow and develop your character, gain peace, heal your body, and allow your mind to rest and reset.

CHAPTER 14

OVERCOMING THE MISCONCEPTION OF FAILURE

14.1 Failure Is Not a Four-Letter Word

There is no success nor failure that hasn't first been affirmed by the mind and upheld by thinking.

Natalie Preci

The mere idea of success or failure is a misconception. We neither succeed nor fail at anything. The idea that we have failed at something comes from the belief that we didn't achieve or get what we set out to get within a set time frame.

However, who decided that if you did not hit your target that this qualifies as failure? Wasn't it just an experience? Were you not just living life on your journey towards your goals?

We all encounter failure in life, and it's not our failures that keep us from achieving our goals but our response to failure itself and our avoidance in correcting it. Failure is not a word we should label ourselves with in a derogatory way, but in a positive light, as it suggests that we are still trying.

You can't fail at something you never try. Every new challenge or life path we venture onto has the possibility of failure or success. Nine times out of ten, our success follows in the footsteps of several failures. Success doesn't come without failure, because it's our failures that teach us the principles upon which success can be built.

Failure should not stop us in our tracks but stir up in us a greater determination to keep pressing forward with the new knowledge and tools we have acquired through the mistakes that led us to fail. Failure is a powerful tool and a great definer of character and grit. Determine to overcome any obstacle that may block you from reaching the heights of success that only you know you are capable of.

I have made many big mistakes, multiple times, in business, lifestyle choices and decisions that did not produce the happiness or financial freedom I had envisaged. In fact, these saw me in an even worse place than that from which I had started. Each choice I made required a financial commitment but an even larger emotional commitment that involved my entire family.

These decisions were, I believed, well thought out and according to my calculations, risks worth taking for the expected positive return on my investment. However, no matter what new business idea I threw myself into or what geographical move I made, I realised that the one common denominator that prevented my success was me.

I thought if I just kept a positive attitude and poured all my effort into every venture, then eventually, something had to pay off.

14.2   Pity Party for One

Little did I know at the time that I was not learning from my mistakes, and I was ignoring the lessons that presented themselves during times of perceived failure. I was more comfortable spending time at my own pity party, where I could bathe in the justification of my victim mentality rather than take responsibility or accountability for my role in the outcome of my decisions. It was much easier for me to find any and every external source to blame for my failure than to take a teaspoon of cement and harden the fuck up.

If I could have stopped the self-defeatist self-talk that continued to bury me further in self-pity, I might have been able to take from my failures, so to speak, a positive lesson, and get straight back up on that horse and try again. Failure has a negative connotation attached to it and represents the opposite of success. But success isn't as black and white as that.

14.3   Failure Identifies Our Weakness

Every successful person you know or hear about has had to overcome failure. To be successful, one must first know one's weaknesses, and to know one's weaknesses, one first must fail. That's why we can never give up but use our failures to identify those areas in which we need to improve and grow. Failure can be such a positive tool in our personal growth and self-mastery, without which success would only be temporary, as we wouldn't have the skills required to sustain our success when the road got tough.

14.4   Personal Growth and Development

Personal growth and the development of oneself are the most important gifts we can take from our failure. Use failure to shine a light on the parts of yourself that are causing blockages on your road to success. Nothing in this world other than ourselves can ever keep us from becoming successful if we have the right attitude and self-belief that comes from a place of humble self-worth. When we come to understand that all we need to be successful is already within us, we can show gratitude and thanks for that which we already have. This is the first step to overcoming all things.

CHAPTER 15

CHASING THE WIND

15.1 Materialism

---

[17] So I hated life, because the work that is done under the sun was grievous to me. All of it is meaningless, a chasing after the wind. [18] I hated all the things I had toiled for under the sun, because I must leave them to the one who comes after me.[19] And who knows whether that person will be wise or foolish? Yet they will have control over all the fruit of my toil into which I have poured my effort and skill under the sun. This too is meaningless.

Ecclesiastes 2:18–19, NIV

The term "chasing after the wind" in scripture has had an incredible impact on my life and the way in which I now view the acquiring of material things for materialistic sake. The New King James Version describes it as vanity and vexation of spirit. Working to fulfil another person's passion, pouring energy into someone else's financial success, is an intolerable way to exist. When are you going to take that energy, which contains immense creative force, and direct it into your dreams?

We use materialistic objects to fill the gaping hole in our life. We work longer hours, give up our annual leave, and drag ourselves to the office when our bodies are aching. All this is so we can make the money needed to repay the bank, to repay the debt we have accumulated by our need to compete within our own social circles.

Do you know that your neighbour doesn't have a nicer or bigger house than you? He just has a bigger mortgage. I don't know many Australians who have $600,000 lying around to pay their house off in full, in cash. They have a mortgage just like you. And if they drive around in a flashy car, then that's sure to be financed also.

How many things do you own that you're proud of? Maybe your big-screen TV or the latest electronics or new furniture for your home? Now which of these did you pay for in cash? I'm guessing you paid by credit card. You see, we own nothing of what we have of a materialistic nature. The bank owns our house, the finance company owns our car, and the credit card companies own our possessions.

We are slaves to our possessions. They keep us under pressure to work harder, longer hours just to ensure the bills are paid on time. We do this because these things create a picture of a satisfying life that gives us a false sense of pride. If you pin all your self-worth on your exterior facade of a wealthy lifestyle when you're up to your eyeballs in debt, you are on a slippery slope. If you lose your job or get sick, missing a couple of scheduled loan repayments, all those materialistic things you believed constituted your worth could be taken from you in an instant. What will you have left when your self-worth is repossessed along with all your possessions?

Why get sucked into consumerism to remain relevant in world that places more value on things than people? Your value is within and something that cannot be taken or repossessed. Do not become a slave to that which you think you own, because you don't own it. It owns you! What you own is your thoughts and your dreams, your desire, passion, and vision. First be grateful for all you have. Then that which you don't have will chase you!

15.2 Madness and Folly

---

¹⁷And I set my heart to know wisdom and to know madness and folly. I perceived that this also is grasping for the wind. ¹⁸For in much wisdom is much grief, And he who increases knowledge increases sorrow.

Ecclesiastes 1:17–18, NKJV

Do you feel you're forever chasing after something you can never catch? And if you do finally catch it, does it fully live up to your expectations? We work most our lives starting from school and university landing that dream job, only to find ourselves lacking.

Whatever it is, it doesn't matter if you're too tired to enjoy it and not able to mindfully experience the present moment. Our lives have become so busy that we don't even realise we're not living at all. There is so much life we miss when we get caught up in a robotic mindset and continue to go about life with our eyes facing downward and our heads stuck in the sand.

We often miss the incredible beauty all around us, and we forget to be happy. When is the last time you stopped to meditate, just clear your mind of all outside distractions, and connect with your body, your breath, your soul, the earth?

When is the last time you woke up at five in the morning, went down to the beach, and watched the sunrise? When is the last time you felt grounded? Can you remember a time when you were truly happy? If so, why aren't you feeling that right now?

Society and the real world in which we live programs and conditions us to a life that is always seeking excitement, adrenaline, and chasing an excess of material things rather than seeking the real meaning and inner contentment that comes from connecting to our higher selves.

15.3   Too Busy to Live

Chase first the things of substance within and all the desires of your heart will seek you out.

Natalie Preci

The world is keeping us so busy working to get the money to spend on more pointless unnecessary things that only give us a rush of pleasure in the moment, most likely due to the release of a short burst of serotonin. These things we work so hard to obtain are momentary and do not fulfil our intrinsic need for profound inner happiness in every moment.

That doesn't mean you shouldn't have money or an abundance of things; it means stop chasing them and let them flow to you by tuning your thoughts into the frequency in which they travel. You will never catch wealth if you are tuned in to the frequency of greed or corruption. You will never catch success if you are tuned in to the frequency of failure. You will never catch love if you are tuned in to the frequency of hate. We must tune our frequency to the channel that is playing the music of our hearts' desires.

You first must recognise the motivation that drives you towards your wants, and if your motivation is not grounded in gratitude, love, and appreciation, you will forever be chasing the wind. The laws of the Universe will scientifically not permit you to catch that which you want when your vibrational energy is emitting the energy that opposes it.

CHAPTER 16

DEFYING THE ODDS

16.1 The Odds Are Never Too Great

By three methods we may learn wisdom: First, by reflection, which is noblest; Second, by imitation, which is easiest; and third, by experience, which is the bitterest.

Confucius

You may be reading this book and thinking that the principles outlined within it may be beneficial to some people but could not be applied to your life because the obstacles you are up against are just too insurmountable to be defied. Well, I want to implore you to reject this thought instantly.

Although I have experienced my fair share of troubles in life, I know there are others who have been dealt a hand much worse than mine, and so unfairly that it makes them query the scales of justice. You may have experienced abandonment, sexual abuse, physical abuse, or been the victim of violent crime—all of which have the effect of leaving you feeling trapped by the terror of emotions that seem to be ever-present in your daily life. One word by a passing stranger or an innocent touch of your arm can reignite all the emotions and feelings from that past event still lingering just below the surface of your calm, cool exterior.

I am not a medical practitioner or a psychologist, but I believe that even the most traumatic events in our lives can be overcome when we are ready to let go of the memories that contain within them the emotional and physical manifestations of those events.

16.2   Two Brothers—One Alcoholic Father

There's an old story about two boys whose father was an alcoholic. They grew into young men. This story relates to the justification we use for the choices we make:

> Twin boys were raised by an alcoholic father: One grew up to be an alcoholic and when asked what happened he said, "I watched my father." The other grew up and never drank in his life. When he was asked what happened, he said, "I watched my father." (Author unknown)

Two boys, same dad, two different perspectives. Your perspective in life will determine your destination.

16.3   You Have A Choice

No matter the traumatic extent of your experiences, it's entirely your choice how you choose to respond. Don't give those experiences more power by entertaining them in your mind. Don't allow them to drive your emotions. Haven't you suffered enough by the actions of others? Is it not time to just let it go?

Letting go of negativity from your past does in no way justify the crimes committed against you. Nor does it absolve the perpetrators of accountability. It does, however, free you from being a victim forever. It gives you the strength to take back control of your life, allowing you to remove the heavy yoke around your neck and find your peace within.

CHAPTER 17

HOW TO REPEL NEGATIVITY AND TOXIC PEOPLE

17.1   Energy-Sucking Vampires

Repelling negative and toxic people isn't easy, as when they encounter positive people such as yourself, they will want to feed off your energy, like blood-sucking vampires. They will hang around and suck the life-force out of you, offloading all their own drama and problems without giving thought to the implications for your state of wellbeing as they spew forth their negative and toxic energy. After this interaction, they go about their day feeling relieved, refreshed, and energised, while leaving you drained, exhausted, and emotionally spent.

You know who I'm talking about! You know those people who seem to lurk around on the outskirts of your life and know exactly the right time to strike. When you're feeling on top of the world, they are there to pull you down. When you are feeling down, they are there to kick you and keep you down.

These people are toxic, and if they are still in your life in any capacity, keep them at a safe distance if you can't remove them altogether. I'm not here to say you should surround yourself with only positive people, because even positive people have bad days. At times, they require help in raising their vibrational frequency. But these are not the ones I'm referring to. I'm referring to the ones who take from you without limit yet repay you nothing.

17.2   Defining Your Boundaries

The fact that you are reading this book suggests that you are a person who is committed to personal growth and development and who strives to maintain a high standard of moral conduct. It also suggests that you have a deep respect for all people, even at times when you may not like them.

My desire to help others was embedded in the marrow of my bones and therefore occurred as a natural impulse, devoid of any forethought. Even when it came to people I knew to be toxic, I was unable to resist the urge to assist them. If only out of mindful respect for my self-worth, I had implemented clear and defined boundaries in my relationships. But at the time, lacking any level of emotional maturity, I found it easier to cut people out of my life completely.

Although setting loving and concise boundaries is the best option, removing toxic people from my life at times was imperative, keeping me committed to my own self-development. As much as I would like to imagine a world where every soul was thoughtful and mindful of others, I have broken free of my delusional bubble of rainbows and butterflies. I now realise that not all people act from a pure and selfless heart. Some possess dark intentions and act in ways that are bankrupt of empathy and understanding.

I have known many of them personally, although they are no longer an active part of my life. Rather a slow learner, I naively sought to believe the best of people. I was quick to forgive, even so kind as to provide justification for others' inability to show kindness.

Well, they are really stressed out now! They are having problems in their relationships. They have that problem child who won't let them sleep. They are really struggling financially. They had a hard road growing up. They lost their loved one and just need time to vent. They don't have anyone else to listen to them.

There is no justification for anyone to treat another human being without respect, irrespective of their circumstance or situation.

17.3   Remaining Steadfast in Your Resolve

If you have people in your life who are not sources of encouragement, love, acceptance, constructive criticism, and gentle guidance, they need to be removed from your life, and if that's not possible, kept at a safe distance. There is nothing more detrimental in your journey through life as those who want to see you fail and go to all lengths to make sure it happens. These people will not only assist in your downfall but find quite a bit of happiness in their triumph. They will not have compassion; they will neither show empathy nor show you any mercy.

Be careful and guard yourself. Be strong and definitive in your resolve to remove these people from your life. The road to attainment is an uphill fight, and you won't get there with baggage trying to pull you back down.

There are many motivating factors that cause people to become toxic in your life. These include jealousy, envy, selfishness, arrogance, and narcissism. You can try to negotiate with these people, but I'm sure you already have. If they haven't gotten the message yet, they probably never will. Surround yourself with positive people who support your dreams and visions for your future.

17.4   If You Are the Smartest One in the Room

If you are the smartest person in the room, then you are in the wrong room.

Confucius

If most people you associate with are not intellectually compatible with you, then it is unlikely you will learn to grow from them. You will most likely end up dumbing yourself down to be accepted and fit in, which is the biggest mistake you could make.

When we associate with people of high intellect, wisdom, creativity, or knowledge, we are inspired to greatness. We are inspired to reach for the highest heights, to challenge our thinking, to become more inquisitive, to expect more of ourselves, and to dare to dream dreams of boundless possibility. You deserve to remain in your harmonious positivity bubble without someone coming along with a pin and popping it. It took you too long to get here.

CHAPTER 18

DISCOVERING TRUE HAPPINESS

18.1   Letting Go of Unhappiness

Wherever you are, be there totally. If you find your here and now intolerable and it makes you unhappy, you have three options: remove yourself from the situation, change it, or accept it totally. If you want to take responsibility for your life, you must choose one of those three options, and you must choose now. Then accept the consequences.

Eckhart Tolle, *The Power of Now*

To obtain true happiness, you must be ready to let go of unhappiness and understand that happiness is not an emotion or feeling; it is an inner state of being. People like to hang on to their sadness as a badge of honour. They share their stories of childhood, enjoying the empathy they evoke with each recital.

You would have heard your dad or grandfather say something like this at some stage while growing up: "When I was a boy, we didn't have electricity. We had to do our homework by candlelight, and we ate bread and dripping for dinner." Well, I have. I have also heard my mum's life story a million times.

Although I detested pity from others and rarely shared my stories, they still circulated in my thoughts on a regular basis and somehow defined me. They became the excuses I used to justify my shortcomings in life.

18.2   Fear of Being Happy

There is something about our human nature that fears being happy. It seems we have this need to hold on to negative experiences just to feel balanced. But who said we ever need to feel sad, lonely, depressed, or unhappy? On the contrary, it is our universal birthright to experience life abundantly, full of wonderful emotions, all the time.

You would have read quotes by famous people that just add to our already unqualified perception of happiness. Like "Happiness isn't a constant" or "Happiness is fleeting" or "Expect only glimpses of happiness strung on a necklace of despair." Really? Why do we accept that the state of inner happiness cannot be achieved or experienced every moment? The society in which we have grown up has conditioned us to believe that being happy all the time is unobtainable and unsustainable—that our way of life keeps us from it. How can we be happy all the time when circumstances require us to feel differently?

For example, you might be going through a divorce or have a loved one who is sick or has passed away. Being happy is not the default state in which you will find yourself. And it's OK to feel sad or overwhelmed with the burdens you are facing. You are not expected to express happiness during these times. However, there is a way in which you can consciously decide to walk through these difficult times on a higher frequency of positive energy, making the journey a little lighter and avoiding the possibility of slipping into a deeper state of negative emotion.

When you don't permit your mind to spiral too far down during these times, the climb back up is not so formidable, and you can resume a positive state of happiness a lot faster. They say time heals all wounds. Imagine being able to shorten the time it takes to get back to living life to the fullest, even after a major devastating event in your life.

Why stay in a place of mourning and grief for years, keeping yourself locked in a place of sadness? It may hurt, and the pain may be palpable for some time, but you have the strength within you to get up and move forward. If you give in to negative feelings, they will overtake you and continue to intensify.

CHAPTER 19

THE CREATIVE FORCES OF NECESSITY

19.1 When We Hit Rock Bottom

Necessity is blind until it becomes conscious. Freedom is the consciousness of necessity.

Karl Marx

There is nothing that will inspire and motivate you more than necessity. It is only when we find our life in a ditch, having lost everything, on our knees with our heads in our hands, that real change is found. It's when we hit rock bottom, having nothing left to lose, no one there to pick us back up, no more excuses left to fall back on, and no one left to blame that we must decide between do or die. It's time to wake up out of our victim mentality and decide to be victorious.

We must find the inner strength and determination arising from our primal instinct for survival that refuses to accept defeat. We must take back the responsibility for our lives that we have handed over to others and use the creative forces of necessity to reclaim our lives. It isn't going to be easy, but it can't get any worse.

The reason you may have found yourself in this place is because you have always taken the easy road; the road of less resistance; the road well travelled. This road may be easy, but you are walking in the footprints of those who have already etched out a path. The road that has easy access also has many exits.

It's time to take the hard road, the one that requires maximum discipline and courage. That's the one you must fight to find, and it has few exits along the way. It's the one that challenges you every moment of every day. Just you and the road! There is no one beside you egging you on. No one in front of you motivating you to pick up the pace. No one behind you challenging your position. There is nobody telling you to go faster, and nobody telling you to stop. Just you!

19.2   Are You Going to Walk Or Run?

The Wright brothers didn't invent the flying machine because they couldn't walk but because they dreamed of flying.

Natalie Preci

So, are you going to walk or run? It doesn't matter either way, because only you know if you're forging ahead. You are in a race for your life where your only competitor is your mind. Is your mind going to let you just casually stroll down that road, setting minimal limits and requiring the least amount of effort? Are you going to let thoughts of self-doubt start to creep in as you look up at the mountain ahead of you?

Are you going to let your perception of the task ahead be impaired by your thoughts? Will you believe that the mountain is just too big, too high, and too far out of your margins of ability? Or are you going to ignore these thoughts of limitation your mind has set, trying to prevent you from reaching the top? Will you take up the challenge with an attitude of *I can*? Decide that quitting is no longer an option and that nothing will stop you until you have marvelled at the view from the mountain's peak.

It's time to break through the boundaries of your ability and grasp on tight to your immeasurable capabilities. This is the mindset required to turn things around in your life and to become a fighter. You must be fearless now, because you're in the fight of your life, but it is a fight you can win if you know your opponent. Who is your opponent? Your opponent is you!

It's all the demons within. The negative energy you feed yourself throughout the day, saying you are hopeless and there is no way back, is a lie! You have the power over your mind to arrest these thoughts of self-defeat. You can do it, and you will, because you wear the scars of battle and you are still here. This makes you victorious already.

19.3   The Hidden Treasures Within

Believe me or not, it's in that dark place where all hope is seemingly lost that you discover the treasures you possess. This is when you can pour out all that sadness, all the pain and disappointment, and redirect it into passion, drive, and desire. This is where you turn the energy created by your necessity into creativity.

Necessity has a powerful creative force attached to it. The most important inventions of this century have all been the child of necessity. If there is no need, then there is no creation.

All things in the universe have been created out of and through necessity. Thomas Edison didn't create the light bulb because he had nothing better to do with his time; he did it because he was probably sick and tired of burning himself with candle wax. The Wright brothers didn't invent the flying machine because they couldn't walk but because they dreamed of flying.

19.4   Don't Wait Until It's Too Late

Who do you know who was overweight all their life and only stopped eating sugary sweets when they got a diagnosis of diabetes? How many people even consider quitting smoking until they get diagnosed with cancer? Why is it we wait? What is it we are waiting for before we are willing to change? Are we waiting for a prognosis of death before we start living every day as if it's our last?

Well, I hate to be the bearer of bad news, but you already have a prognosis of death of the physical form. The only certainty in life, is death. Any day you wake up could be your last. We don't know what date will be inscribed on our headstone.

Have you ever considered why people who have near-death experiences honour every minute of their existence? Because their life was plucked from the hands of death. Because they know what it feels like to be faced with their own mortality and have felt what it's like to look back on life with regret. They've experienced lying in a hospital bed, praying, and wishing for one more month, one more day, one more hour, one more minute, one more second to make their life count.

Why wait until it's too late? Why put off living every second as if it's your last? We need to learn how to value every moment we have on this earth and utilise each with intent and purpose.

Every day is a gift, and one day the choice to live or die will be taken out of our hands. Right now, though, we still have a choice. If we are alive and have blood coursing through our veins, we have time to change our destiny.

Your end date has not yet been determined, so start now in creating a legacy for your children, for your grandchildren and their children. A legacy is eternal, your energy footprint in the sands of time that will serve as a record of your stint here on earth. You have unique creative qualities that can enrich the world, qualities that only you possess. It's your birthright as well as your obligation to express them in a way that only you can. The only difference between you and those you admire is that they believed they could and gambled everything on it, going all in.

When are you going to place a winning bet on yourself? Don't wait for others to increase the odds; you must raise the stakes. No second-guessing, no fear of losing. You must go all in.

19.5   Who Will You Let Steal Your Dreams?

How many times have you thought of inventing some new gadget only to see it the following month in the shops? Have you wanted to slap yourself for not doing it first when you see it making millions of dollars being traded on the stock market? It was your idea! The only trouble is, you failed to act. You had the idea, believed in its profitability, but neglected to follow it through to implementation.

Remember, thought inspires action. Without action, our thoughts and ideas remain just that. They never become a tangible reality for us until we turn them into action. What talent or idea have you had for the longest time but procrastinate taking the action required to see it materialise? We all have one if not many creative ideas that could not only see us living out our dreams but provide us with a substantial stream of passive income. Try not to focus on the enormity of the project or get caught up in the intricacy of the details. Just take the first step.

That first step will inspire you to take the next, then the next, then the next. The energy you emit will start to gain momentum, and before you know it, you will see your dreams realised. A journey of a million steps starts with just one. So, are you inspired yet and ready to take your life to new heights? If so, buckle up, because you are on the express train to attainment.

Follow the motivational tools in this book, and you will see yourself achieving all you can imagine in a very short time frame. This is not a long and winding road; it is short and straight if you have the right mindset and willingness to get up, shake off all the negative self-talk, and allow yourself to become the best version of you.

CHAPTER 20

REWRITING A PAINFUL PAST

20.1   Factory Reset

The first thing I required to rewrite my past was a factory reset—clearing out all files, programs and settings and starting fresh. We need a reboot and to start reprogramming our minds with a new set of instructions that are in accordance with our dreams, desires, and beliefs. If your childhood memories evoke feelings of sadness, anger, or disappointment, these negative emotions are still contributing to your present reality.

Unless you can learn how to rewrite your painful past by letting go of these emotions, you will carry them with you throughout your entire life, never experiencing any depth of aliveness. They will continue to arise in every situation in your life without warning—and sometimes without you being consciously aware. They can affect your relationships, work life, family life, and overall state of mind, and can lead to serious conditions of mental illness and addiction.

When you think about your past, what really is it? Look back at your past as a collection of movie scenes that resulted from the way in which your brain processed the information you were exposed to and the sensory feelings you experienced.

20.2   Memories

Our brain cannot see. Only our eyes can. So what information are our eyes transmitting to the brain to create an image or memory? Light. Our eyes absorb light in spectrums of colour and intensity. Our brain analyses and processes that light and records it as a mental image. This image creates our memory. This image or memory does not have any effect on our current reality. It remains on our hard drive, and we can access it at will if we choose.

But as you will no doubt be aware, when we access these memories, we also access the emotions that went along with them that were saved along with the memory. So, if the memory is a bad one that carries with it negative emotions, why bring it back into your conscious present-day awareness? Better to delete it from the hard drive altogether and rewrite a more positive one. "Easier said than done," I hear you say. Well, yes and no.

It's easy if you are at a place where you are ready to let it go and don't require it anymore to justify yourself or your life. It will be hard if you're not quite ready for change and you want to hold on to it so just in case you don't thrive, you can use it as an excuse. It's your choice whether you wish to remain trapped by your past or are ready and willing to write a new memory.

Since you are still reading, I'm going to say you fall into the second category and are ready to do whatever it takes to kiss your painful past goodbye.

20.3   Change Your Emotional Response to Your Past

Remember, it is not the memory that holds us back. It is our emotional response to it. To change our negative response, we must first rewrite the memory. If you do this with the most prominent times in your life that altered you, they will begin to lose their ability to cause you pain. The bitterness, anger, or disappointment you have carried all these years towards those who wronged you will no longer have the impact it once did. You have rewritten their wrongs and therefore rewritten the emotional reaction they initiate.

Nothing will justify the delinquencies of the human heart that as children we can fall victim to, or the wrongdoing that is committed against us, but we can choose whether we wish to let them define us anymore. This process of rewriting my past took no more than a couple of days, and the effect on my attitude, disposition, and general state of happiness was immediate.

Don't go another day feeling trapped in your past and remaining in the emotional state it evokes. You've suffered enough. It's time to be happy.

CHAPTER 21

HOW TO CREATE A NEW PARADIGM

21.1 A New Chapter in Your Life

Today is the day you are starting a new chapter in your life. Today, everything is changing in your life, starting *now*! As we touched on in the previous chapter, one of the most powerful tools we have at our disposal is our imagination. Our imagination gets put on the shelf as we age; it's something we had so much of as children, but many of us lose the ability to tap into this boundless resource.

As children, we don't set any limits on our dreams. We dream big! We don't apologise for or doubt that we can do anything or be anything we want. We believe we can fly! If you ask every kid what they want to be when they grow up, not one will *ever* say, "Average!" They don't imagine being stuck in a job they hate, going to work every day dreading every minute in a cubicle, daydreaming about somewhere else they'd rather be. They don't see themselves getting up at five every morning to go to a cleaning job for minimum wage. They don't imagine their adult lives as anything less than extraordinary.

What happened to that child in us who wanted to be an astronaut, pilot, fireman, dancer, singer, or movie star? What happened to your dreams of greatness? As we walk through life, we seem to forget about the things that used to fill our entire bodies with exhilaration and cause us to become animated about the future.

We forgot to dream. We forgot to want more. But why? Why does this happen, and what is it about us that we can so casually let go of our ambition and the discipline required to flourish? Well, you will be relieved to know that you did not do this on a conscious level, and there are many factors that contributed to your diminished capacity to visualise your dreams.

These factors probably started to influence you as early as five years old, when you would have had the awareness of others' assessments of your strengths and weaknesses. For example, you may have heard your parents say, "Oh, he really struggles with math; I guess he's just not going to be one of those academic types," or "She is so smart, but don't get her to dance—talk about uncoordinated." I hope your parents never said this to you, but you may have heard similar characterisations on the playground from peers or in the classroom from your teacher. Whoever it was, these character assumptions took up residence in your subconscious and began to write your story, forming your beliefs and setting subconscious limitations. Your abilities never changed, but your faith in them did.

Your subconscious mind has no power of itself to pick and choose what it wants to believe. It acts as a servant to your mind and follows your orders without question. It will seek out and attract the energy and frequency produced by the beliefs it was programmed to accept as its reality.

If your subconscious has been wired to believe that you are, for instance, no good at sports, then every time you try to play a sport, you will most likely suck at it, no matter how much you try. Even if you are determined to master the skills of the game and put in a considerable amount of time practising, your limitations have already been established. You may see some improvement in your game, but it will only be temporary, as your subconscious will eventually revert you to your default programmed state of sucking at sport when it realises you are not manifesting in accordance with its guidelines.

No matter how strong your conscious efforts have been, you will be overruled by your subconscious paradigm. So, let's change it! We must erase your existing belief system and reprogram your subconscious to start seeking out new frequencies and create a new paradigm.

CHAPTER 22

LAWS OF THE UNIVERSE

22.1 Law of Attraction

The law of attraction is something you may already know about or have heard about in recent years. It is a theory that has been made famous by books such as *The Secret*, which was featured on *The Oprah Winfrey Show* and turned into a documentary.

I had watched the episode on Oprah some years back and thought it was a nice idea for those who maybe didn't know God and needed something to believe in, but for me, I had my faith. It seemed on the surface like a similar concept to prayer. Ask and you will receive. Ask for what you want, believe with all your heart that God will provide it, and with faith, your prayers will be answered.

I believed that the law of attraction was just another way scientists had found to explain away and oppose the power of prayer. It seemed my faith had blinded me from exploring any other way of understanding my existence that didn't match up with scripture or acknowledge the God of the Trinity as the one true God. All this talk about us being God and the Universe being God and Mother Nature being God was just too loose a theory for me to get on board with. But now I can clearly see the difference between the two.

With religion, I was required to ask first, then have faith, and then wait. But with the law of attraction, it is very different. I first must believe that I already have it and wait for it to manifest. "They don't sound too different," I hear you say. Well, let me explain further.

When you ask for something, there is an expectation that you will be told either *yes* or *no*. The point of asking for something means you don't already have ownership of what you are asking for. Therefore, you are requesting permission to be granted it. Once you have made your request known, you then have to decide if you believe you are worthy of receiving your request. This is where things get interesting. How many of us feel worthy when it comes to deserving anything from God?

I know when I prayed for something, I would always end my prayer with, "If it be your will." With that statement, all my faith in getting my prayer answered flew out the window, as all the doubt as to whether it was God's will to answer my prayer crept in. That left me wondering if my prayers weren't answered because they weren't in accordance with God's will or if I just wasn't deserving enough. Was it that my faith wasn't strong enough? Whatever it was, it frustrated me. Why were there so many variables involved? Why was it not as simple as, "Ask and you shall receive"?

So then we come to the law of attraction and the absoluteness of its effectiveness in having every prayer answered. There is no doubt about your worthiness, because anything and everything you could ever dream of is already yours.

We are all inhabitants of this earth and have equal claim to its abundance. If we are all sinners, then what makes one person more entitled than the next? Who decided that of the trillions of dollars in circulation, you should be poor and your neighbour rich? Does an immigrant working fifteen-hour days cleaning windows of an office building deserve to be paid an amount consistent with his physical output? Why is the CEO sitting in an office getting paid a hundred times more annually than that cleaner? Has the cleaner worked harder or the CEO?

Regardless of who worked harder, each worker is paid for his time. Whatever work we do, our time is given a dollar value. Don't we all deserve an equal value to be attributed to our time?

Money, contrary to popular belief, is not the root of all evil, nor is the pursuit of it. If you think of it logically, it is simply paper with no real value in and of itself. And nowadays, paper currency isn't even the most common form of money. We have moved to the more convenient plastic card, our mobile phone, and even crypto currencies such as Bitcoin.

But even with all these different forms of money, whatever way you look at it, money is simply numbers punched into a computer. If money is just numbers, then it becomes easier to visualise. It's when we try to visualise massive amounts of it in its paper form that we question our ability to have it. Most of us want what money can buy us and do not pursue it for extravagance and excessive materialism. It is to buy what is priceless: our freedom. *There are no rich slaves!*

Money gives us the freedom to follow our dreams, the freedom to enjoy the finer things in life, the freedom to spend more time with our children, the freedom to contribute to charitable causes, the freedom to go on holidays, and the freedom to be free from the hardship of poverty.

Money in the hands of an evil heart will produce evil, but money in the hands of a good heart will produce love. It's only our belief that we don't deserve to be wealthy or happy or successful that stops us from achieving it. This universe that we call home is so full of riches and opportunities just waiting for us to reach out and pluck them straight from the realm of probability into our reality.

You see, everything you want already exists in the form of energy. When you understand this, it will all make sense. Going back to the theory of quantum physics, it teaches us that all matter and all things on a quantum scale are, in their raw state, pure energy.

CHAPTER 23

POWER OF THOUGHT

23.1   Our Thoughts Are What We Become

I have touched on the power of our thoughts in previous chapters, but because this is such a game-changer, I'm dedicating an entire chapter to helping you understand it so there's not a shadow of doubt left in your mind.

Our thoughts are the very thing we become. It's that simple! No grey area! No maybes! If our thoughts have determined what we have become, then doesn't it make sense they are the very same thing we will need to use to become the person we want?

When you think of your mind, which is the creator of your thoughts, what is it you think of? If you say your brain, that's not entirely correct. Your brain is the processor of thoughts created by your mind, but unlike the brain, the mind exists and operates independently from the brain yet the two are inseparable. This is also the same when it comes to our consciousness and subconscious.

23.2   A Powerful Message—Rubin "Hurricane" Carter

It reminds me of a movie I once saw called *The Hurricane*. It impacted me greatly and left me in awe of the enduring nature of the human spirit and our mind's ability to transcend even the tallest prison walls. *The Hurricane* is a true story based upon the life of a man named Ruben Carter. This man was in his early twenties and primed to become the heavyweight boxing champion of the world. It seemed he had done the impossible. He had become a successful man of colour during an era where racism and hatred was at its peak.

After spending much of his childhood in and out of juvenile penitentiaries, his vision of the future had been bleak at best. However, when he was able to control the anger, frustration, hatred, and injustice inside him, he was able to unleash it with powerful force in the ring. And he did, becoming a professional boxer in 1961.

Sadly, the crimes of his youth and his criminal convictions continued to plague him and would eventually see him wrongfully convicted of a triple homicide. He was sentenced to life in prison in 1966, which sealed his fate and obliterated his dreams of becoming champion of the world. Hurricane Carter served twenty years, locked in a cell for twenty-three hours a day, before being acquitted of the charges against him.

Just try to imagine how it would feel to be physically confined and isolated for so many years. You would feel hopeless and start to question what it is to be human, no longer possessing any perception of reality. Because in that cell, the only reality you know is the four walls that encompass you. The world outside the prison no longer exists to you; the only thing that exists is your fading memories of what it was.

So how do people survive in these extreme psychologically crippling environments? Well, most don't. But there is always the exception.

Following Rubin Carter's initial incarceration and in the early years of his imprisonment, I imagine he experienced a range of negative emotions, the most destructive of all being, hate. This would have been a living hell, to realise he had no one there to direct his hate and bitterness towards, and the only person suffering from their effects was him. He is quoted as observing, "Hatred and bitterness and anger only consume the vessel that contains them. It doesn't hurt another soul."

For him to be able to endure his sentence, he had to stop fighting his situation. He had to accept that there were certain things he couldn't change and amend his way of thinking, which was keeping him locked in—not locked in prison, but locked in the prison of his mind, thoughts, and emotions.

Haven't we all trapped ourselves at some point in a prison of our own making, letting our thoughts and emotions keep us from any true freedom? There is an unmistakable connection between Rubin Carter's prison and the one we sentence ourselves to.

We are all captive to our thoughts, and it's our choice as to whether they remain within the emptiness of their four walls or break free and wake to the fullness of our existence.

23.3   Our Thoughts Can Set Us Free

Only thoughts can keep us trapped in any one version of ourselves, or in the reality in which we exist. As we allow different thoughts in, the old ones must leave. When are we going to start welcoming thoughts into our mind that have the power to create visions of greatness?

We need thoughts that are uplifting, positive, and inspiring—thoughts that motivate us to be free of our current state of reality and start believing in a new one. Aren't we the ones who hold all power of creation in our life?

Yes, the power to create a life of design and purpose is ours. When you can accept this fact, your life will start to flow like water down a river of infinite possibility, producing gentle ripples of creativity and raging waters of ingenuity. It's a wonderful ride for those who choose to take it and bathe in its electrifying energy.

CHAPTER 24

THOUGHT-INSPIRED ACTION

24.1 The Thought Cycle

Do you know that every thought you have inspires action? It's like Newton's Third Law of Action: "For every action, there is an equal or opposite reaction." Our thoughts and words elicit a similar response. What we think, whether positive or negative, will in that moment lead us to action, and in turn create the relevant emotion or feeling that action evokes. The feeling and/or emotion the action creates then compounds the original thought, starting the cycle over.

Have you ever got up in the morning and thought about going for a run? You had all the intention of going, and the thought even inspired you to start getting dressed. Then out of nowhere another, a thought popped into your mind: *I'll just check my emails.*

The thought of checking your emails took you away from your original thought of going for a run, and now you have stopped getting dressed and are on the couch with your phone or laptop. Then you see you have a Facebook message. Without thinking, you check that too, and before long, the whole idea of going for a run has escaped your mind. You are now on the couch and have either forgotten about the run or given more space in your mind to something else, most likely something that requires less effort than running.

This is something we do every day without consciously being aware of it. We listen to and act on every thought that enters our mind without quantifying it as to its importance or asking whether it is in line with our beliefs or desires.

We subconsciously go through the day on autopilot, submitting to each thought we have, even if it is not consistent with what we want. Therefore, people struggle with addiction, never able to break free from it. You may make that huge decision to quit, having so much determination and will power, only to find yourself giving in to the addiction at the mere thought of it.

During the days of my addiction, I would go for months at a time without ever thinking about my drug of choice. Then one day, I would find myself stressed out or feeling miserable, and the thought of having the drug would pop into my mind. Not long after, I would begin to get excited about the physical feeling and emotions associated with the high. At times, my body would have a physical reaction from the mere thought of having it. I would begin to get excited, and my whole mood would change. I could start to imagine my misery being lifted.

I can assure you, once that thought entered my consciousness and I started to entertain it, nothing could stop the intense desire and determination running through me to get it. And I did get it, every time! That's thought-inspired action at its worst.

Imagine for a minute that we could take this principle and turn it around for our benefit. Imagine that we could use our positive thought to create positive inspired action, then positive emotion and/or feeling. The positive emotion and feeling associated with the positive action we took would then ignite positive thinking. Suddenly, we have changed the cycle. Negative and positive, they are both the same. You must choose which one you want to follow.

The only problem with this is we tend to go through our lives with default thoughts to most experiences we encounter. Imagine if, in your current position, wherever you are in your life or whatever state of emotion or circumstance you find yourself in, you could just change one thing—a thought, action, or emotion—and it would start the wheels turning in a positive direction.

It may seem difficult if your situation or circumstance makes it hard to think positively. Maybe you are struggling with depression, illness, addiction, relationship problems, or situations that you don't feel you have the power to change. I can tell you with 100 per cent certainty that you can change your current reality by creating a new way of thinking.

The fact that you are reading this book means you are ready for change and willing to do whatever it takes to start living a life that motivates you to get out of bed every morning with hope, inspiration, and passion.

24.2   Changing Your Thoughts

Changing your thoughts when your mind is fixed in a negative pattern requires a rewiring of your brain. This is done by making a choice to let go of all the negative thoughts going through your mind of the past, present, and future.

Imagine you have amnesia and any thoughts of the past that are not making you feel good are wiped clean. You have no memory or any past hurt or pain, disappointment, or regret. Now, imagine you only have today to live, and the future is irrelevant; therefore, you can let go of any anxiety about tomorrow. What you have left is today, this moment, to decide how you feel.

Right now, say to yourself: "Today is going to be the best day of my life!" It doesn't matter that you may not believe it or that your circumstances don't align with this statement. Saying these words is the first step to making that statement a reality. It's not because your physical reality has changed, but because your internal reality has now been altered. If you continue to wake up every day reaffirming this statement, your subconscious will begin to reprogram your hard drive.

To fast-track the process, I encourage you to listen to guided meditation and daily affirmations.

24.3 Changing Your Actions

Changing your actions is the most difficult thing to do, as it requires first a change in thought or emotion. It is impossible to act differently than you usually do without first having a mental or emotional shift in that direction.

Just as you can't get your computer to cook you dinner, you can't get your physical self to do something it wasn't programmed to do. If you look at your subconscious as if it were the hard drive of a computer and your conscious mind as if it were the RAM, it will help you to understand that you cannot just ask the RAM for information that was not first downloaded to the hard drive. It will come back and say, "Sorry, your search returned no results." That's like the way we operate.

If your subconscious has no recollection of a positive action you take in this circumstance, it will simply revert to your default action. Or if the action doesn't align with your subconscious programming, it will reject it instantly. Therefore, before we can create positive action, we first must reprogram our hard drive, instructing it to accept these new actions as new capabilities overriding our existing limitations. Our emotions also can affect our actions. You will know this because we experience this every day.

Our emotions have a massive impact on how we act. When sad or depressed, we don't want to go out or speak to anyone; we most likely just want to get in bed, turn all the lights out, and huddle up in a ball of misery. When angry, we tend to lash out physically, or our anger will lead us to our favourite addiction with the intention of calming us down. That may be smoking, drinking, drugs, food, exercise, or whatever else it is we rely on to take the edge off.

What about jealousy or revenge? These emotions can have the most devastating physical response, as they can lead to gossip, hatred, murder and all sorts of destructive behaviour, leaving a path of intense negative energy in their wake.

So, to avoid these negative actions, we need to be aware of the negative emotion that is causing them. Until we can recognise the emotions causing unwanted negative action, we will not be able to learn how to change our behaviours. Address the cause, not the response. Trying to cure the outward manifestation of emotion is a futile venture. Only when we tackle the emotional trigger can we alter the output of that emotion.

24.4   Changing Your Emotions

Changing your emotions requires an extreme amount of conviction, but it can be done by first identifying the emotion you want to experience, which will probably be the opposite of what you are currently feeling. You need to invoke a precise recollection of a time or thing that had once aroused these feelings. Once you have that vision clearly in your mind, focus on it, shutting out all other thoughts and sounds around you. Imagine yourself back in that same moment.

How did you feel? How did you look? Were you smiling? Did you have a sense of gratefulness to be alive? Whatever it is, try to meditate on that feeling, and you will start to experience it in the present. It will take practice, but in time, you can create any emotion you wish at any time you want no matter what your circumstances.

When you master this technique, you will find the cycle of your life beginning to change to positive.

CHAPTER 25

AFFIRMATIONS AND MEDITATION

25.1   Positive Affirmations

Affirmations can be negative or positive, and they form a vital component of every day as we affirm those things about ourselves or our reality in that moment, solidifying a preprogrammed belief or creating a new one. For the most part, affirmations will strengthen a pre-existing belief more effortlessly than they will create a new one. Our subconscious mind will not reject affirmations that are in line and in accordance with ideals that have been previously programmed, but new beliefs require new programming.

Whether aware of it or not, you use affirmations in your daily life already and probably don't understand that these affirmations may be the thing that is holding you back in life or keeping you in bondage to a behaviour pattern. When we use affirmations to affirm negative thoughts, feelings, or emotions, we manifest them into our present or future reality. The frequency of such affirmations and the conviction in which they are affirmed determines how soon and to what degree they will manifest.

The positive affirmations you recite will only be effective if they align with your subconscious paradigm. If they do not, your conscious mind will reject them and continuously revert to that which it has been programmed to believe. You may have noticed this in your own life when you have consciously decided to eat healthy and exercise more. You may have talked yourself up, told yourself you will only eat green leafy plant food and go to the gym five nights a week. You may have decided to start on Monday, having all intentions of sticking to your guns this time. If you were really determined, you might have been able to honour your commitment to change for a week or maybe even a month, but mostly we soon realise that our strong will and initial determination to achieve such goals were somehow not enough, as we fall quickly back into our old ways.

It's like New Year resolutions. How many times have you decided to make big changes on New Year's Eve, only to find that within the first week of January, you are already struggling to uphold them, and before long, give up? This is not entirely your doing. If you are unaware of the powerful opposition you are coming up against that is resistant to change, your subconscious mind will fight at every step to have you continue in the negative patterns in which it has always operated.

This is not because your subconscious wants to work against you. It doesn't have the ability to make decisions independently but must only act as your servant, ensuring that you stay within the parameters of what it recognises. Affirmations can be used subliminally by advertisers, politicians, and perpetrators of propaganda by using a suggestive form of affirmations to control our thoughts and actions to their benefit.

25.1.1 Advertisers

Advertisers use positive suggestions that make you believe in what they are selling. Even though you already know they exist and can reliably predict what you have to purchase and the approximate cost of these items, they still continue to bombard you with advertisements on TV and fill your inbox with the latest one-dollar discounts. They know that if their products are constantly in your conscious thought, there is a probability that you will act on them. If they can get you in the door to buy just one thing, you are likely to walk out with more. That's the intention of positive persuasion.

25.1.2 Politicians

Politicians use this same principle during campaigns when one of their gifted writers comes up with a catchy slogan and repeats it in the media, on merchandise, and in speeches. They will ensure that their target audience jumps on the bandwagon by chanting the slogan time and time again. It is a system that works because the more we hear something, the more we start to believe it.

25.1.3 Propagandists

People who promote propaganda certainly have knowledge of the workings of the subconscious mind. One of the greatest perpetrators of propaganda of all time was Hitler. Through his continued repetition of his anti-Zionist persuasion, he was able to poison the minds of many average, everyday people and have them commit the most horrific crimes that they otherwise would have never conceived they were capable of doing.

Through the barrage of lies he propagated, he was able to convince the world that the mass genocide of Jews, Blacks, and minority races was a great idea for humanity at large. Here are some famous quotes that confirm this theory:

- "Make the lie big, make it simple, keep saying it, and eventually they will believe it."—Adolph Hitler
- "If you tell a lie big enough and keep repeating it, people will eventually come to believe it.—Joseph Goebbels
- "A lie told often enough become the truth."—Vladimir Lenin

25.2   The Lies We Tell Ourselves

Terrible, isn't it, what others do to plant seeds into our heads for their selfish gain? But is it any different from what we do to ourselves? Don't we lie to ourselves all the time? Our human brains process on average over 60,000 thoughts a day. We have thoughts constantly racing through our minds, chattering nonstop and filling our heads with mostly unnecessary garbage.

What are your thoughts telling you? Are they lying to you by saying you're not good enough, not strong enough, not smart enough, not rich enough, not brave enough, not skinny enough, not pretty enough? Well, if they are, then tell them to shut up right now, because you are being lied to, and it's time for the lies to stop.

This is the moment when you take back control of your thoughts and reject the accusations of your conscious judge, because you are innocent of all charges. Only you have the power of attorney over your mind, and only you can protect yourself from letting it sentence you to a lifetime of regret.

You must replace the lies you have spoken about yourself with the truth, and to do that, you must first acknowledge the lies. This should prove relatively easy as you become receptive to your thoughts and begin to have more mindfulness as to what thoughts and beliefs you will entertain.

When you start this technique, you will quickly be able to pull yourself up when a negative self-belief creeps in. When this happens, acknowledge the thought, let it go, and immediately replace it with the opposite affirmation. If you walk past a shopfront and see your reflection in the window and suddenly think, *Oh I look so fat today!*, correct yourself in that moment by saying, *I am so grateful for this body. It has served me well, and it is beautiful.* It may be hard at first, and you don't have to believe it; just say it enough times and it will form a new truth.

Not only that, but according to the universal law of attraction, the physical world must begin to outwardly exhibit this new truth. Repeat this technique without exception and be amazed at the immediate way in which it affects your state of being. You will instantly feel a rush of confidence and control, knowing that you *do* have the power within you to change. Don't allow one more negative self-thought to enter your conscious mind without counteracting it with a positive one.

This will begin the reprogramming of your belief system and start to alter your current perception of who you are as you begin to transform into the person you have always known you are. Give yourself permission to be the person you were created to be. Free yourself from the matrix of your mind and take dominion over your reality. We have gotten off to a great start, but let's take it to the next level.

25.3   Morning Affirmations

Dr. Phil is famous for saying, "It takes 1,000 *Atta boys* to erase one *You're an idiot*." For every time you have told yourself you're an idiot—for instance, let's say the thought crossed your mind once a day for just five years—that's 1,825 times you have consolidated that idea. So, if it takes a thousand times of hearing *You're smart* to erase just one *You're an idiot*, you are going to need to hear it 1,825,000 times.

Obviously, this is an extreme example, but I wanted to show you how important it is that you start to listen to positive affirmations daily until that affirmation takes hold. Invest in a pair of good-quality headphones, as they are going to become your best friend and constant companion in the days ahead and for the rest of your life. Find some morning affirmations or motivational videos that connect with your needs on YouTube and make the time every morning to listen to them for a minimum of one hour, even if it means getting up early.

This will not be an issue within a week, as you will find yourself with such a renewed passion and zest for life, you'll be up before your alarm goes off, I guarantee you. On waking in the morning, before doing anything else, find yourself a quiet place, free from any distractions. If you can, I recommend you get outside the house, whether on your patio, the beach, or a local park. The reason for this is that when you are outside, you are more connected to the earth's energy and can also absorb the beauty of your surroundings.

Clear your mind of any thoughts of the day ahead or any negative thoughts or feelings from the previous day. Just be in the moment, permitting yourself this time, a time just for you. It's OK—you deserve it, and you are going to need it to achieve all the things you have to get done that day. Now put on your headphones and let yourself start to experience the emotions and feelings associated with the affirmations you're listening to.

These new positive emotions will birth into positive thought, and before long, into positive action. Try to listen as much as you can throughout your day. If you work, listen on your lunch break and in the car driving to and from work. If you're a stay-at-home mum, put them on while you're cleaning the house or working in the garden. The more you listen, the faster your life will start moving in the direction that reflects your true identity.

25.4   The Art of Meditation

The art of meditation has been practised by humanity since the beginning of all human consciousness. Those who have experienced it will understand that it is the gateway to our higher self and connects us with the source consciousness of the universe. Meditation allows you to train your conscious mind to experience the soundless depths of your true self by blocking out the myriad of thoughts that involuntarily dominate your mind.

Meditation is the art of connecting with your body and deliberately commanding it into a state of profound rest. There you can release tension, stress, anxiety, worry, and all negative thoughts, feelings, and emotions. It is a place of surreal peace that brings forth a reservoir of living energy, wisdom, joy, and creativity.

Meditation is something I have never been into and always looked upon as the most pointless, selfish waste of time imaginable. I looked upon those who did yoga as hippie New Age types who weren't in touch with reality. Yet again, my assumptions were so wrong.

I have found meditation in all its forms the most rewarding, energising, and uplifting thing I have ever experienced. In the quiet, restful place of meditation, I found everything I ever searched for, needed, or wanted. In that place, I could connect with an energy so palpable, so tangible, that I could feel it permeate every cell in my body. My mind was taken from a conscious state to a state of awakening of my mind's eye, which could see so clearly my place in the universe and instantly understand my connection to it.

When you can shut out all distractions and be still, you can hear and feel the vibrational energy of your heart beating as you inhale and exhale each breath. Your mind, body, and spirit simultaneously drift into a blissful state of euphoria. Honestly, what else can give you that? No drug has ever made me feel so high and so free from the restraints of the physical world around me.

By meditating consistently, we begin to align our energy with the energy of the universe and manifest anything in the physical world we can possibly think of. Whatever it is we seek to manifest already exists in the form of energy; we simply need to tune in to the frequency, and we can attract the manifestation of that energy into our lives.

CHAPTER 26

NEW LIFE BEGINS

26.1 Relinquishing My Ego Self

For my new life to begin and for me to move into my future with renewed faith, strength, intention, and purpose, I had to grieve the death of my ego. My ego had been like a toxic friend that kept me bound to an identity that wasn't reflective of my authentic nature. It had tied me down and locked me into a false representation of my abilities and limitations.

When relinquishing my ego, I was able to redefine myself based on my inner guide and intuition that freely flowed to me when submitting my mind, body and soul to a place of rest and meditative silence. Inner peace is just that; it comes from within and is not contingent on the absence of external noise, struggles, or trials, but amid such things, you can find calmness in your heart.

It is easy for me to say such things, but living a life that is a testament to such teachings is where the rubber meets the road. I'm not going to say it's easy! I'm not going to tell you that with a few affirmations and meditations, your life is going to be perfect, because that's not the endgame.

A perfect life is subjective. Life will always be a series of moments, days, and years filled with variable portions of trauma, grief, heartache, financial difficulties, troubles, and strife for each one of us. Only we know what difficulties we must overcome. Only we know the struggles we may currently be facing. These things may not be in your ability to change. However, you can change the way in which your mind perceives them and whether your emotional response is a positive or negative one.

If you continue to drag your old mind and old thinking into a new day, then you will continue to have the same old experiences. If you want a new life, then you must have a new mind. Your mind must be changed. Your thinking must be renewed. Your thoughts must be mastered. Unless you want to relocate to the isolated highlands of Nepal and become a monk, then life will happen. The only thing you can change is you.

When you go within, embracing all parts of yourself with loving kindness, the unconditional love that you are can be realised. It is a love that resonates through every cell of your body and resides in all things contained in the universe. We have been born out of love, and it's love to which we will once again return.

You are a beautiful masterpiece—in this moment of your life, a blank canvas. Paint your dreams and visions with brushstrokes of vivid colour, your imagination your only limitation.

When we enter the void of Sacred Silence, we enter the infinite.

Namaste

www.ingramcontent.com/pod-product-compliance
Lightning Source LLC
Chambersburg PA
CBHW050912260726
48660CB00001B/165